```
TA   Howell, Steven K.
174     Introduction to
.H69 AutoCAD Designer 1.1
     Steven K. Howell.
1996
```

Introduction to
AutoCAD® Designer 1.1

Introduction to AutoCAD® Designer 1.1

Steven K. Howell
Northern Arizona University

PWS Publishing Company

I(T)P An International Thomson Publishing Company

Boston • Albany • Bonn • Cincinnati • Detroit • London • Madrid • Melbourne
Mexico City • New York • Paris • San Francisco • Singapore • Tokyo • Toronto • Washington

 PWS PUBLISHING COMPANY
20 Park Plaza, Boston, Massachusetts 02116-4324

Copyright © 1996 by PWS Publishing Company, a division of International Thomson Publishing Inc.

All rights reserved. No part of this book may be reproduced, stored in a retrieval system, or transmitted, in any form or by any means -- electronic, mechanical, photocopying, recording, or otherwise--without the prior written permission of PWS Publishing Company.

AutoCAD Designer and AutoCAD are registered trademarks of Autodesk, Inc.

I(T)P™
International Thomson Publishing
The trademark ITP is used under license.

For more information, contact:

PWS Publishing Co.
20 Park Plaza
Boston, MA 02116

International Thomson Editores
Campos Eliseos 385, Piso 7
Col. Polanco
11560 México D.F., Mexico

International Thomson Publishing Europe
Berkshire House 168-173
High Holborn
London WC1V 7AA
England

International Thomson Publishing GmbH
Königswinterer Strasse 418
53227 Bonn, Germany

Thomas Nelson Australia
102 Dodds Street
South Melbourne, 3205
Victoria, Australia

International Thomson Publishing Asia
221 Henderson Road
#05-10 Henderson Building
Singapore 0315

Nelson Canada
1120 Birchmount Road
Scarborough, Ontario
Canada M1K 5G4

International Thomson Publishing Japan
Hirakawacho Kyowa Building, 31
2-2-1 Hirakawacho
Chiyoda-ku, Tokyo 102
Japan

Library of Congress Cataloging-in-Publication Data

Howell, Steven K.
　　Introduction to AutoCAD Designer 1.1 / Steven K. Howell.
　　　　p.　　cm.
　　Includes index.
　　ISBN 0534-95070-1
　　1. Computer-aided design. 2. AutoCAD Designer. I. Title.
TS174.H69　1995　　　　　　　　　　　　　　　　95-45805
620' .0044' 02855369--dc20　　　　　　　　　　　　CIP

Sponsoring Editor: Jonathan Plant
Production Coordinator: Robine Andrau
Marketing Development Manager: Nathan Wilbur
Manufacturing Coordinator: Wendy Kilborn
Assistant Editor: Ken Morton

Cover Designer: Julia Gecha
Production: Editorial Services of New England, Inc.
Cover Image: Greg Taylor
Cover Printer: New England Book Components, Inc.
Text Printer: Courier/Westford

Printed and bound in the United States of America
95 96 97 98 99 -- 10 9 8 7 6 5 4 3 2 1

Table of Contents

CHAPTER 1—DESIGNER FUNDAMENTALS

INTRODUCTION	1
PARAMETRIC CAD	2
THE DESIGN PROCESS	4
LOADING DESIGNER	6
A SIMPLE EXERCISE	7
END OF CHAPTER SUMMARY	15

CHAPTER 2—BASIC 2-D GEOMETRICAL CONSTRUCTION

INTRODUCTION	17
END OF CHAPTER SUMMARY	31
EXERCISES	32

CHAPTER 3—UNDERSTANDING CONSTRAINTS AND CONSTRUCTION GEOMETRY

INTRODUCTION	37
RELATIONSHIPS BETWEEN CONSTRAINTS AND DIMENSIONS	38
USING DIFFERENT COMBINATIONS OF CONSTRAINTS AND DIMENSIONS TO DEFINE A PROFILE	45
USING CONSTRUCTION GEOMETRY	46
END OF CHAPTER SUMMARY	51
EXERCISES	51

CHAPTER 4—CREATING A 3-D SOLID MODEL FROM A 2-D PROFILE

INTRODUCTION	55
END OF CHAPTER SUMMARY	66
EXERCISES	66

CHAPTER 5—CREATING 2-D VIEWS FROM A 3-D MODEL

INTRODUCTION	71
CREATING AND EDITING VIEWS	72
HOLE NOTES	82
USING DESIGNER'S AUTOMATIC CROSS-SECTIONING FEATURES	83
CREATING AUXILIARY VIEWS	85
CREATING DETAIL VIEWS	86
END OF CHAPTER SUMMARY	86
EXERCISES	87

CHAPTER 6—ADVANCED 3-D CONSTRUCTION: A CHAIN RIVET EXTRACTOR 91

INTRODUCTION	91
WORK FEATURES: PLANES, POINTS, AND AXES	99
END OF CHAPTER SUMMARY	111
EXERCISES	112

CHAPTER 7—USING 3-D SWEEPS AND BASIC PARAMETRIC EQUATIONS 117

INTRODUCTION	117
DEFINING GLOBAL PARAMETERS	118
BUILDING SWEEPS	119
EDITING GLOBAL PARAMETERS	128
END OF CHAPTER SUMMARY	129
EXERCISES	130

CHAPTER 8—ASSEMBLY MODELING USING PARAMETRIC RELATIONSHIPS 133

INTRODUCTION	133
END OF CHAPTER SUMMARY	148
EXERCISES	149

Preface

New computer tools have significantly changed the role of engineering graphics during the last few years. One tool, parametric feature–based CAD, allows engineering graphics to go beyond the role of just documentation and communication of design solutions. Parametric CAD systems, such as *AutoCAD Designer,* allow an engineer to actually build a "virtual prototype" of a design idea or concept and subject that model to various "what if" scenarios. This virtual prototype can quickly be modified as the design solution is refined and implemented.

Drafting and descriptive geometry have been the sole medium for communicating engineering design ideas for nearly 200 years. As computer technology has developed during the last decade, engineering graphics instructors have begun to look at alternative forms of graphical communication. With the advent of computer-aided design (CAD) systems in the 1980s, drafting boards were replaced by electronic tools. These early CAD systems were essentially two-dimensional "electronic drafting boards." CAD systems speeded up the production and revision of engineering drawings but did nothing to change the basic two-dimensional nature of engineering graphics. During the 1990s the field of engineering graphics evolved to incorporate 3-D geometric modeling. One significant barrier to implementing the new 3-D solid modeling paradigm has been the limitations of computer hardware and software. Until recently, CAD systems capable of creating and manipulating 3-D solid models were slow, required expensive hardware, and were not always easy to use. A breakthrough in CAD systems occurred in 1994 when Autodesk introduced *Designer,* the first full-featured parametric CAD system that operates on low-cost personal computers.

I hold the opinion that a parametric-based CAD approach to introductory engineering design graphics offers significant advantages over a traditional approach. A parametric CAD–based methodology more closely parallels the engineering design process than does a traditional graphics approach to graphical design representation. Traditional CAD is focused more on the mechanics of geometric construction than on the representation of design solutions. Parametric CAD allows a student to concentrate on understanding the design process and the result of that process, rather than on the details of drafting. Yet with its automatic drafting features, *Designer* can be used to easily construct conventional orthographic drawings. Conventional 2-D engineering drawings can be "taken off" the 3-D solid model. *Designer* is a quicker and easier way to document and model engineering design solutions than are traditional methods.

Introduction to AutoCAD Designer 1.1 is written as a tutorial-based student manual. This book can be used as part of a course in engineering design, in conjunction with an engineering graphics course, or for independent self-study. This manual covers all the features of *AutoCAD Designer* and presents them in an easy-to-follow step-by-step approach. *Introduction to AutoCAD Designer 1.1* starts with a simple 2-D example to illustrate basic concepts of parametric dimensioning and constraints. The simple 2-D exercise is expanded in subsequent chapters to illustrate advanced 3-D construction and *Designer*'s automatic drafting features. The book concludes with an advanced example, illustrating concepts of parametric relationships and simple assembly modeling.

Introduction to AutoCAD Designer 1.1 was written to meet the following objectives:

- To introduce fundamental concepts of parametric feature–based solid modeling
- To present *AutoCAD Designer* as a tool to be used in the larger process of solving engineering design problems
- To provide an introduction and training in *AutoCAD Designer* in a format suitable for self-learning.

A *Designer* solid model can actually be constructed and edited with a minimal working knowledge of AutoCAD. Therefore, I have not attempted to cover AutoCAD commands in depth. For the student who is unfamiliar with or new to AutoCAD, this text includes "If You're New to AutoCAD" boxes, which give an introduction and/or review of the basic AutoCAD commands needed to construct a *Designer* model.

The Appendix provides an alphabetically ordered reference to all of the *Designer* commands.

Acknowledgments

This book would never have been realized without the contribution of many individuals whom I would like to acknowledge.

First, Jimm Meloy, from Autodesk's Education Department, gave me the initial "kick in the pants" to get this project started. Jim Purcell and Rodger Payne, also from Autodesk's Education Department, provided me with support and encouragement during the months of writing and rewriting.

Many thanks go to the engineering students at Northern Arizona University. They were the guinea pigs who gave me valuable feedback and constructive criticism as the rough manuscript was being refined. Special thanks go to mechanical engineering student Greg Taylor, who generated most of the end-of-chapter exercises and many of the ideas for the examples used in the text. Mechanical engineering student Rob Bannerman helped formulate the introductory concepts.

I am grateful to the reviewers listed below for their suggestions and help:

- Robert Kelso, *Louisiana Technological University*
- Robert Mabrey, *Tennessee Technological University*
- Mustafa Tossi, *Pennsylvania State University*

The publishing expertise of several people at PWS Publishing Company deserves special mention, especially that of Jonathan Plant, Kathleen Wilson, Robine Andrau, and Monica Block.

Last but not least, I wish to thank my family—Debra, Joshua, Rachel, Gabriel, and Benjamin—for their patience and understanding during the long hours spent in front of a computer.

Steven K. Howell
Northern Arizona University

Chapter 1

Designer Fundamentals

Introduction

AutoCAD Designer represents a new paradigm, or way of doing engineering graphics. It is a tool that goes beyond generating engineering drawings. In the 1970s engineers found they could be more productive in problem solving by using a new tool, the pocket calculator. This tool did not change the "problem solving process," but allowed engineers and engineering students to solve problems more quickly. In the same way, Designer represents a new way of creating geometric models of engineering design problem solutions and will allow engineers to be more productive at solving design problems.

Designer works inside AutoCAD, using familiar AutoCAD drawing and editing commands. However, Designer does not require a detailed knowledge of all the various tools and features of AutoCAD. Complex three-dimensional models can be created with only a basic understanding of AutoCAD drawing and editing commands since Designer uses its own. Designer does not replace conventional CAD, but gives you enhancements that allow three dimensional geometrical models of a design solution to be produced with relative ease. Designer solid models are built by using features that define the model in terms of its functionality, rather than by geometrical entities such as lines, arcs, circles, etc. A Designer model is created by defining the behavior of the design and the relationships between the various geometrical elements comprising the design.

In addition to creating 3-D solid models with greater ease, Designer has automatic drafting features which allow for relatively simple creation of conventional two-dimensional multiple view drawings from a 3-D solid model. Because the 2-D views are closely associated with the 3-D model, you can edit or change a feature on one of the 2-D views, and the 3-D solid model will be correspondingly modified. Likewise, any changes you make to the 3-D model will automatically generate the appropriate changes in your 2-D drawings.

A traditional CAD system is not an effective design tool. Traditional CAD is optimized for creating detailed drawings, not for solving design problems. AutoCAD Designer does not change the design process; you still generate ideas, visualize, analyze, draw, and relate geometry and equations. However, it does change how quickly you work, how quickly you explore design alternatives, and how quickly you document the results.

The process of creating a Designer model is considerably different from creating conventional CAD drawings. With conventional CAD, the drafter worries about geometrical entities: circles, arcs, lines, polylines, etc. The drawing is composed of individual unrelated entities, and any changes to the drawing necessitate editing and/or redrawing all features of the drawing. The creation of a Designer model is much like solving a design problem: you start with an idea (a sketch), and follow a step-by-step method (the design process), to refine that idea and produce a finished product (a complete 3-D solid model and associated engineering drawings).

The real payoffs with using Designer are when editing and changing a drawing. Because a Designer model is a complete geometrical representation of the physical object, any changes or modifications to one element in the model affect all other elements. For example, you may define a hole as being a certain distance from two edges. If you move these edges, the placement of the hole moves accordingly. Therefore, modifications to the model can be done very quickly, eliminating the need to redraw and modify the entire drawing.

The lessons presented in this text assume that you have a basic understanding and knowledge of fundamental AutoCAD commands for drawing, editing, plotting, and working with files. When this text requires the use of an AutoCAD command, the command will be described in a special box, *"If you're new to AutoCAD."* If you're already familiar with the AutoCAD command, just ignore this box and continue with the lesson.

Parametric CAD

Parametric based CAD systems use terminology and jargon that may seem foreign at first, but are actually based upon simple underlying concepts. Designer is called a **parametric feature based** solid modeling tool. **Parametric** means that parameters, or properties of the model, are used to define the model instead of simple dimensions. **Feature based** means that a Designer model is comprised of features, rather than unrelated geometric entities. Designer features are industry standard objects such as fillets, holes, or chamfers. For example, a counterbore hole is a feature in a Designer model, rather than a collection of lines, circles, and cylinders. By changing a few values in a graphical dialogue box, the counterbore hole can be changed to a countersunk hole, and Designer will make the appropriate modifications to your model.

So what does parametric CAD add to conventional CAD? First, you do not need to be concerned with the initial sizes of geometrical objects, you need only sketch in the basic shape. Designer will "clean up" the sketch and allow you to specify later on the exact dimensions and geometrical relationships in the object. Designer geometry is driven by the dimensions and geometric definitions that you specify, so complex relationships are maintained between drawing elements; that is, circles remain tangent and lines stay parallel or perpendicular. Parametric CAD will automatically reshape the drawing as you change dimension values. You can write equations defining the relationship between elements on the drawing. For example, the diameter of a hole can be specified as a function of the diameter of a shaft. Therefore, the hole diameter is automatically updated in response to a change in shaft diameter. Designer automates many tedious drafting tasks, particularly those associated with producing multiple view drawings from a 3-D solid model. With a few clicks of the mouse you can automatically generate ortho, auxiliary, details, or isometric views of your model on a conventional 2-D engineering drawing. Because Designer maintains associatively between these 2-D views and the 3-D model, any changes made to the model are reflected in the 2-D views.

Definition of Terms

The first step in understanding parametric CAD is to understand the new jargon and terminology. To the uninitiated the terminology may seem intimidating, but the underlying concepts are simple and merely an extension of the way engineers solve design problems. The name, parametric CAD, refers to the use of parameters to define a model of a design solution. A parameter is a property of a system, whose value determines how the system will behave. The parameters, or properties, defined in a Designer model determine the geometry of the model you are creating. Parameters can be either mathematical equations, dimensional values, or geometric constraints such as parallel lines, concentric arcs, tangencies, etc. A Designer model is defined and created in terms of the relationships between the various elements comprising the model. With a conventional CAD system you create the spatial relationships between the geometric elements such as lines, arcs, circles, points, etc. Designer's parametric dimensions define or drive the geometry of a parametric CAD model—you change a dimension and the entire model changes! The parametric definitions can also be relationships such as, "side A is twice as long as side B," or "side A is perpendicular to side B."

Designer uses two types of constraints to define the geometry of your model; **parametric dimensions (numeric constraints)** and **geometric constraints**. Geometric constraints are parameters that define the geometrical relationships between entities in the model such as tangencies, orthogonality, perpendicularity, etc. When you first create a Designer model, geometric constraints are assigned automatically, based upon the initial sketch. Designer's ten basic geometrical constraints are listed in Table 1-1. Numeric constraints are similar to dimensions. When you specify a numeric constraint to a Designer model, you are defining the size of the feature or entity. It is important to understand the difference between conventional dimensions and numeric constraints (or parametric dimensions): numeric constraints define the geometry of the model, while conventional dimensions merely indicate a measure of the size of the geometry. For example, a Designer hole feature is defined by a parametric dimension which specifies the diameter of the hole. If you change the value of this parametric dimension, the hole size will also change. A conventional AutoCAD dimension, in contrast, will only indicate the diameter of such a hole, and does not define or specify the hole properties. In other words, constraints *drive* the model, while dimensions are a measure of the size of the model.

A **profile** is a two-dimensional view of your model, seen from some base direction in 3-D space. Designer automatically creates a profile from the sketch you construct initially. The sketch is made of standard AutoCAD two-dimensional entities such as lines, arcs, or circles. After creating an initial sketch, Designer analyzes your sketch and applies geometric constraints based upon how you drew the sketch. Designer automatically closes endpoints, aligns parallel entities, snaps lines to vertical or horizontal positions, and aligns centerpoints of circular features. These geometric constraints then become the basis for the numeric constraints (parametric dimensions) which you can assign to the model. Each constraint, whether geometric or numeric, has a symbol automatically assigned to it by Designer. These symbols may then be used algebraically to define further relationships. For example, the equation **D2 = D1/2,** states that the dimension identified by the symbol **D2** is equal to the one half the dimension value represented by **D1**. This is an example of an **algebraic numeric constraint.**

Table 1-1 *Designer Geometric Constraints*

Symbol	Constraint
H	entity is horizontal
V	entity is vertical
L	entities are perpendicular to each other
P	entities are parallel to each other
T	entity is tangent to circle or arc
C	collinear entities fall on the same line
N	arcs or circles have the same centerpoint
X	entities have the same X value
Y	entities have the same Y value
R	circular entities have the same radius values

A Designer model begins with a **sketch** representing the approximate size and shape of a 2-D profile of a 3-D model. A Designer sketch can be quickly created with standard AutoCAD drawing commands, with no regard to dimensions, closing end points, tangencies, or orthoganality. If you're an experienced AutoCAD user, it may seem strange to not use the usual AutoCAD drawing aids to make sure your sketch is "perfect." Once you've completed this sketch, special Designer commands are used to "solve" this sketch and create a clean 2-D profile. Designer automatically assigns geometric constraints when it "cleans up" the sketch. Lines that are "nearly" vertical or horizontal are automatically snapped horizontal and vertical, arcs and circles are aligned concentrically, endpoints are closed, and lines are realigned to become parallel.

The Design Process

Solving design problems is usually an iterative process. This means that the perfect solution to a design problem does not exist. As the solution evolves, you will find yourself continually modifying and refining the design. Using conventional CAD to document the solution to a design problem, any changes or iterations may require completely reconstructing the CAD drawing. Designer, though, lends itself to modeling the design process and any changes or iterations made in the design solution. The process of creating a Designer model parallels the process of solving an engineering design problem.

Solving an engineering design problem requires a sequential methodology or process. The **engineering design process** is a series of discrete steps used to arrive at a solution to a design problem. A Designer model is also created in a series of discrete steps in much the same way an engineer solves a design problem. There is an ongoing debate amongst engineers regarding the appropriate "model" to represent the design process. It is not the purpose of this text to become involved in that debate. We will discuss the creation of a Designer model in terms of the widely accepted Ideation-Refinement-Implementation model of the design process.

Step One: Define the Problem

This first step in solving a design problem may seem obvious, but the problem must be clearly and unambiguously defined. A clear statement of the problem will determine the approach and form of the solution.

Step Two: Form and Sketch Your Ideas

The solution to an engineering problem begins with creative ideas. These are often the product of a brainstorming session. A pencil sketch is used to record these ideas, which are later made into CAD drawings. A Designer model also begins with a two-dimensional sketch. Using Designer, the engineer will also create a quick sketch, not worrying about dimensions, orthogonality, connections between line segments, parallel features, etc. Designer will automatically analyze this sketch and "clean it up" by closing endpoints, aligning parallel lines, snapping entities to horizontal and vertical angles, and applying any other needed geometrical constraints.

Step Three: Refine the Sketch

The next step in the process is to "refine" the sketch, adding dimensions and defining the geometrical relationships between entities. Designer uses two types of constraints to define your model: numeric constraints and geometric constraints. Numeric constraints are analogous to dimensions: they are numeric values defining the distance or size of a feature. Numeric constraints determine the size of the object or feature. Geometric constraints define the geometric characteristics and relationships of pieces of geometry. For example, the geometric constraints define whether a line is horizontal, vertical, perpendicular, or parallel to another line. Geometric constraints also apply to circular features and determine tangencies, center locations, and radii. Designer uses both types of constraints to fully define the model. The geometric constraints are automatically assigned based upon Designer's analysis of the sketch you created in the previous step. You then add the numeric constraints, but also have the capability of editing the pre-assigned geometric constraints.

Once you have a 2-D fully defined profile, special 3-D features of Designer can be used to turn it into a 3-D solid. Designer can create a solid by extruding, sweeping, or revolving the profile. This task is simplified through "intelligent" dialog boxes which indicate graphically how each operation will affect the resulting 3-D object. Complex models can be created from the basic 3-D solid by defining additional "profiles" and performing the Boolean operations (cut, intersect, or join) to create complex 3-D objects. Features such as holes, countersinks, fillets, and chamfers can be added to the model through the use of graphical dialog boxes.

Step Four: Modify the Design

By definition, design is an iterative process. The design engineer will be required to modify the model in response to these iterations. With a non-parametric CAD system, this usually requires reconstructing the entire 3-D model to accommodate even minor design changes. Defining the 3-D model parametrically allows the engineer to make changes and have the software automatically update all related features and geometry.

Step Five: Implement the Solution

The final phase of the design process is implementation, which refers to the testing, construction, manufacture, and documentation of the solution to the design problem. Designer has an important role in several of these activities.

The documentation of your design solution must be clearly communicated with others. Designer has the capability to automatically generate multiple view drawings from a 3-D solid model. Orthographic, auxiliary, isometric, detail, and cross-sectional views can be quickly created with a few clicks of the mouse using graphical dialog boxes. Since bi-directional associativity is maintained between the 3-D model and the 2-D drawings, any changes to the model are automatically reflected in the views presented in paper space. This capability is one of the big payoffs to using Designer for engineering documentation.

A Designer model represents a complete unambiguous 3-D model of your design solution. Therefore, it is relatively simple to use this model as input for other important engineering applications such as finite-element analysis, rapid prototyping (using stereolithography or CNC applications), and photorealistic rendering.

Loading Designer

AutoCAD uses what we call "open architecture." This means that other features or programs written in the C programming language can be added to AutoCAD. AutoCAD is the "engine" and features not available can be added on top of the engine. Designer is one such program. As a Designer user you don't need to worry about the details of writing and implementing this program. You only need to know how to load and link the Designer program with AutoCAD.

When Designer was installed on your system, one of the installation options was to have Designer loaded automatically every time you start AutoCAD. Generally, this is the preferred way to install Designer, so you don't have to worry about loading the program every time you want to use it. If your installation was not configured to automatically load Designer, then you'll have to manually load the Designer menu and program before you can use the software.

Step One: Load the Designer Menu System

There are several ways to load a new menu in AutoCAD, but we will use the right hand side screen menus. First, select **Utility** from the root AutoCAD screen menu. Then, under the **Utility** screen menu, you will select the **Menu** option. AutoCAD should load a dialog box showing various menu files. Select the menu titled **adesign.mnx**. This will automatically place a new menu structure on AutoCAD. You will see a new menu option called **Designer**, which replaces the previous **Model** menu.

Step Two: Load the Designer Program

The second step in loading Designer is to load the Designer program into AutoCAD. There are several ways to do this, but the easiest method is to use the Designer pull-down menu. Select **Designer** from pull-down menu system at the top of the screen. Under the **Designer** pull-down menu, select the **Utilities** option. This will open up another pull-down menu and you should select the **Load Designer** option. An alternative is to start AutoCAD and enter (**xload "adesign"**) at the command line. Designer is now loaded and ready to go.

A Simple Exercise

To illustrate how easy it is to create a 3-D model, including orthographic views, you will construct a model of the object shown in Figure 1-1.

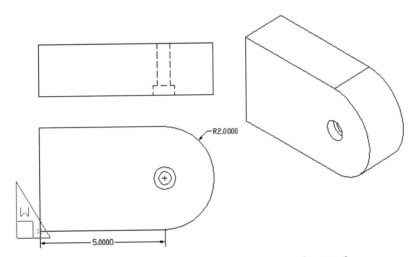

Figure 1-1 *Designer 3-D model of mechanical part*

Step One: Create a Sketch Representing the Profile

Creating a Designer model closely parallels the engineering design process. You begin your model by drawing a "rough" 2-D sketch of the profile of the object. Unlike conventional CAD, you don't need to concern yourself with getting the sketch perfect. Lines do not have to exactly connect or be orthogonal. Although you should draw the profile "close" to the intended size of the object, you don't need to worry about exact locations or dimensions. The dimensions are added at a later point in the design process. Since the dimensions you add are "parametric," they will actually be used to define the geometry of the object. Because they're parametric dimensions, you can easily change them, which will also modify the geometry of the model. For example, if you change the radius of an arc, the entire model geometry is updated to reflect the new radius.

To create this object, use an AutoCAD polyline, or AutoCAD lines and an arc, to construct the shape shown in Figure 1-2.

8 Designer Fundamentals

If You're New to AutoCAD: Polylines

A **polyline** is a convenient way to draw combinations of straight lines and arcs. A polyline is constructed by entering the command **pline**↵ at the command line prompt. You can also create a polyline by using the pull-down menus:

Draw>Polyline>2D

AutoCAD will prompt you with:

Current line width is 0.0000
Arc/Close/Halfwidth/Length/Undo/Width/<Endpoint of line>:

The command enclosed within the <> brackets is always the default command. To use one of the other options you can type the first letter (capitalized) of the command. To create a series of connected straight polylines, simply click the left mouse button in response to the **<Endpoint of line>:** prompt. When the figure is complete, you will type Close or just C to complete the set of polylines. If you make a mistake, type Undo, or U to undo the previous polyline segment. To create the arc shown in Figure 1-2, type **A** to switch to arc mode. AutoCAD will prompt you with:

<Endpoint of arc>:

You can continue to create connected arcs by click the left mouse button in response to this command. Type **L** to switch back to straight line mode.

You can complete the polyline and return to the **Command:** prompt by typing ↵.

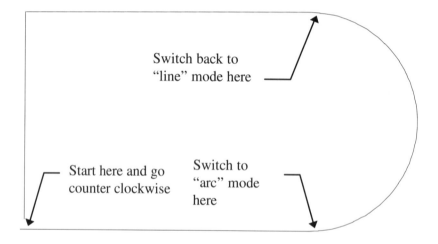

Figure 1-2 *Designer "sketch" of part*

Notice that the lines are not necessarily orthogonal and the endpoints are not connected. Designer will perform these clean-up operations in the next step.

Step Two: Create a Designer "Profile" from Rough Sketch

Next, you will use the Designer **adprofile** command to "solve" and clean up the sketch you created in Step 1. You can type this at the **command:** prompt, or use the Designer pull-down menus.

Select **Designer>Sketch>Profile**

Designer will prompt you to select the object(s) for the profile. You can use an AutoCAD Window to select all the objects, or you can select them individually using the left mouse button. If you used a polyline to draw the sketch, you only need to pick a single line on the sketch and the entire sketch will be selected. As you select objects for the profile, they will become highlighted (a dashed line). After selecting all the features of your sketch, press ↵ to complete the selection.

Designer will then analyze the sketch and apply the certain rules to "clean it up." Lines that are "nearly" horizontal will become horizontal, and "nearly" vertical lines will become vertical. Arcs connected to lines will become tangent to the lines. Endpoints will be connected to make a closed figure. (Chapters 2 and 3 will look at how Designer constrains geometry in more detail.) Your profile should look like the one in Figure 1-3.

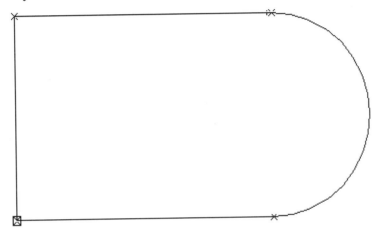

Figure 1-3 *"Cleaned up" Designer profile*

Notice how the **adprofile** command places an x to mark connecting segments. The square indicates the **fixed point** where you started constructing your sketch. The fixed point is the location where your sketch is always anchored in space. As you modify the geometry, the fixed point never moves.

Step Three: Add Parametric Dimensions to the Profile

Now that the geometry has been defined, you are ready to specify dimensions, or the exact size and shape, of the profile. Remember that you did not initially construct the sketch to any specific size or dimensions. Unlike conventional AutoCAD dimensions, Designer parametric dimensions will actually drive or define the geometry. When you constructed the profile in Step 2, Designer gave you the message:

```
Solved under constrained sketch requiring 2 dimensions /
constraints
```

This message indicates that before the profile is fully defined you need to specify two dimensions. For this simple example, you can see that you need to specify either the vertical and horizontal lengths, or the horizontal length with the radius of the arc. Once these dimensions are defined, the profile is considered **solved** or **fully constrained**.

To add these dimensions use the **adpardim** command, or from the pull-down menus:

Select **Designer>Sketch>Add Dimension**

Designer will respond with

Select first item: *Pick near the midpoint of the horizontal line.*

Select second item: *Pick outside the line. This point will be the location of the dimension placement.*

Because you pick a line that is constrained by Designer to always be horizontal, Designer automatically determines that this dimension must be a horizontal linear dimension. Designer will indicate at the prompt the current value for this dimension. The value displayed will be the length of the line that you used to construct the initial sketch. You can either accept the default value or enter a new number. For this example, you want the horizontal length to be **5** units, so enter the value **5↵**. Notice that the geometry automatically updates to reflect the new length of 5 for the horizontal line. Designer will respond with:

```
Solved underconstrained sketch requiring 1 dimensions /
constraints
```

Looking at the sketch you can see that the one required dimension is the vertical distance or the radius of the arc.

Select first item: *Pick anywhere on the arc.*

Select second item or place dimension: *Pick a point outside the arc.*

Again, Designer dimensioning is context sensitive, so a radial dimension is automatically specified. Designer indicates the current dimension value in < > brackets. You have the option of accepting this value, or entering a new one. The number indicated is the radius you used when first constructing the sketch. For this example, specify a value of **2 units**. Designer will respond with:

```
Solved fully constrained sketch.
```

Press ↵ to complete this operation. The radius of the profile will change to reflect the value of 2 which you specified for this parametric dimension. Your complete profile should look like the one shown in Figure 1-4.

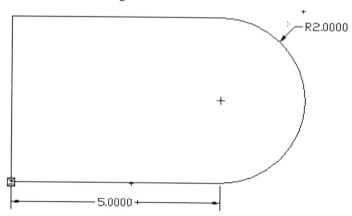

Figure 1-4 *Completely dimensioned Designer profile*

A Simple Exercise 11

Step Four: Refine and Modify the Model, Making It 3-dimensional

Now that you have a completely defined 2-dimensional profile, you will **extrude** it to create a 3-dimensional solid. The extrude operation simply adds a specified thickness to the planar profile in a direction normal to that profile. Finally, you will drill a counterbore hole through the part, concentric to the arc.

Before performing the extrusion operation, you should view the part from an isometric view. From the Designer pull-down menu,

Select: **Designer>Part Viewing>Iso**

You will see the completed 2-D profile from an isometric view as shown in Figure 1-5.

Next, you will turn this 2-D profile into a Designer 3-D extruded solid. From the Designer menu,

Select: **Designer>Features>Extrude**

A Designer extrusion dialog box will appear. Enter a distance of **2** and accept all other defaults. The dialog box should be completed as shown in Figure 1-6.

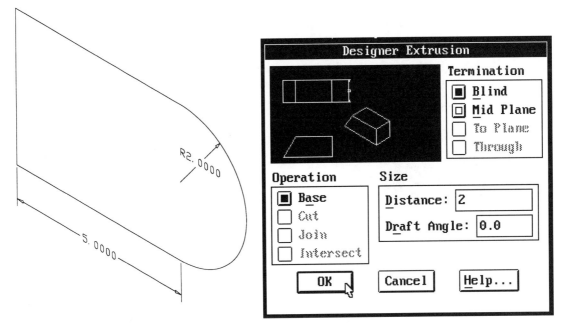

Figure 1-5 *Isometric view of 2-D profile*   **Figure 1-6** *Designer extrusion dialog box*

After completing the dialog box click **OK.** The profile will be extruded to a thickness of 2 units. The dimensions will disappear after extrusion. The complete solid should appear as Figure 1-7.

12 Designer Fundamentals

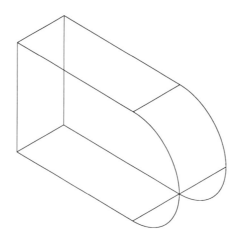

Figure 1-7 *Complete 3-D solid model*

Next, you will add a hole to the front face, with a placement concentric to the arc. Unlike conventional CAD, a Designer hole is a complete feature, rather than unassociated lines and circles. Designer uses graphical dialog boxes to create features such as holes. From the Designer pull-down menu,

Select: **Designer>Features>Hole**

You will see the Designer hole dialog box. Notice that the type of hole is indicated graphically in the dialog box. You have a choice of a through, counterbore, or countersink hole. We will use a counterbore hole and accept the default values for all dimensions. Complete the dialog box so that it looks like the one shown in Figure 1-8.

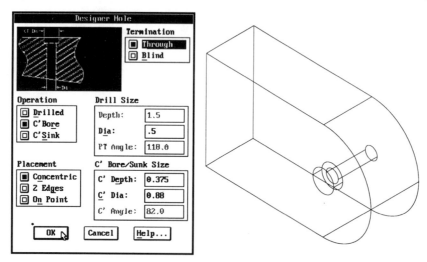

Figure 1-8 *Designer hole dialog box* **Figure 1-9** *Complete model with counterbore hole*

The hole should be drilled entirely through the object and placed concentric to the arc. The diameter is .5 units. Accept the default values for the counterbore depth and diameters. After completing the dialog box, click the **OK** button. Designer will prompt you for the hole location.

X/Y/Z/Ucs/Select work plane or planar face: *Select any point on the curved edge of the face on which you want the hole to be placed. The option will place the hole on a planar face perpendicular to the axis of the selected curved edge.*

Select concentric edge: *Simply select another point on the same curved edge.*

The hole will now be automatically drilled through the front face of the object. Your model should look like the one shown in Figure 1-9.

Step Five: Implement the Model

The final step in the design process is implementing the design solution. With a parametric CAD system, the implementation step consists of producing a set of engineering drawings from your 3-D solid model. With a traditional CAD system, you start with a set of orthographic drawings. In contrast, parametric CAD starts with the 3-D solid model and ends with a set of 2-D engineering drawings. The orthographic, detail, and isometric drawings are automatically created from the solid model. Designer has advanced automatic drafting capabilities, which allow the engineer to quickly create these traditional drawings from the 3-D model. Because Designer supports **bi-directional associativity**, the drawings can be modified and the model will correspondingly be adjusted or you can make changes to the 3-D model and see corresponding modifications in the 2-D drawings. For example, you could edit the 5-inch linear dimension in one of the orthographic views and the 3-D model will be updated automatically. Because the Designer model represents a complete part, rather than unrelated geometric entities, the engineer does not have to erase and redraw the entire model when making design changes.

To illustrate how easily you can create conventional drawings from a Designer model, you will create a top, front, and isometric view of the model. From the Designer pull-down menu,

Select **Designer>Drawing>Create View**

You will see a dialogue box showing all the various view-placement and type-of-view options. The initial view in any drawing must be the base view. All other options are grayed out. Other views are then taken from the initial base view.

Figure 1-10 *Designer Drawing View dialog box*

14 Designer Fundamentals

Complete the box so that it looks like the one shown in Figure 1-10. If you like, you can type a view label in the appropriate box. Pick **OK** when finished. Designer will answer with the following prompts:

Xy/Yz/Zx/Ucs/<Select work plane or planar face>: *Pick anywhere on the front face of the part (the face where the hole is drilled).*

Next/<Accept>: *If the correct (front) face is highlighted, press ↵. Otherwise, use the Next option until the correct face is highlighted.*

X/Y/Z/<Select work axis or straight edge>: *Pick the line that is to be aligned with the X-axis in the drawing view. For this part, pick the bottom line.*

Rotate/<Accept>: *You will see an icon representing the X- and Y-axes of the drawing you are creating. You can rotate the X- and Y-axes for the drawing view by typing* **r**. *Press ↵ when the icon aligns properly.*

Designer next switches to a blank screen which represents a blank sheet of paper. You are now prompted to locate the new view on this blank sheet of paper.

View center: *Pick a point in the lower left side of the screen. You can continue to pick a location until the view is in the proper place. Once you're satisfied, exit this command by pressing ↵.*

For the base view you just created, Designer will remove hidden lines and show any parametric dimensions that are parallel to this view. Your drawing should look like the one shown in Figure 1-11.

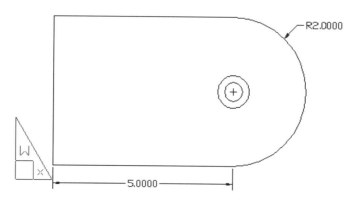

Figure 1-11 *Base drawing view of part*

You will repeat the above process to create a top view and an isometric view of the model. Use the **Designer>Drawing>Create View** menu to create these views. Now that you've created the base view, the other options are not grayed out. Select the **Ortho** view and accept the defaults in the Designer **Drawing View** dialog box. Designer will prompt you with:

Select parent view: *Pick the base view of the part that you just created.*

Location for orthographic view: *Pick a location above the base view you just created for the top view. You can move the ortho view around until it's in the right location. Press ↵ when you're satisfied.*

You can press ↵ to repeat the **Create View** command and bring the dialog box back up. The last view you will create is an isometric view of the part. Check the **Iso** option in the dialog box. Then choose **OK**. Designer will prompt you with:

Select parent view: *Pick the base view of the part.*

Location for isometric view: *Pick a location above and to the right of the base view. You can move the iso view around until it's in the right location. Press ↵ when you're satisfied.*

Your drawing should look like Figure 1-12. Notice that the hidden lines are removed in the isometric view.

End of Chapter Summary

You've just created a simple three-dimensional solid model. Using Designer's automatic drafting features you made a fully associative drawing. If you'd needed to edit any of the dimensions in the drawing, the model would have been simultaneously modified to incorporate those changes. This lesson only introduces you to the basics of parametric CAD. In future lessons you'll create much more complex 3-D models and explore the powerful editing and automatic drafting capabilities of a feature based parametric CAD system.

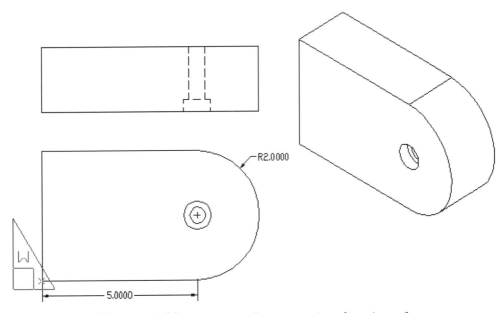

Figure 1-12 *Completed engineering drawing of part*

Chapter 2

Basic 2-D Geometrical Construction

When you have completed this lesson you will be able to:
1. **Create a two-dimensional "sketch" of a profile**
2. **Use Designer to "clean up" this sketch into a "profile"**
3. **Apply Designer's geometric constraints to this profile**
4. **Apply parametric dimensions (numeric constraints) to this profile**
5. **Show, add, and delete geometric constraints**
6. **Understand the relationship between geometric constraints and dimensions**

Introduction

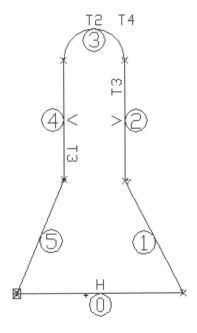

Figure 2-1 *"Ice Scraper" profile*

This lesson illustrates how to use Designer for basic two-dimensional geometrical construction. You will create a 2-D profile of the ice scraper shown in Figure 2-1. This lesson illustrates the important concepts of **geometric constraints** and **parametric**

18   Basic 2-D Geometrical Construction

dimensions (numeric constraints). Geometric constraints define the geometrical relationships between elements of the model. For example, line 0 in the above figure has been given a horizontal geometric constraint, indicated by the **H** symbol. This means that as the model is edited, this line will always remain horizontal. Line 4 has been given a vertical constraint and is constrained as tangent to the upper arc. The symbols **V** and **T** indicate these types of constraints. The other constraints are numeric, or dimensional. You will assign the numeric constraints or dimensions as you work through this tutorial. A direct relationship exists between geometric constraints and dimensional constraints. Both type of constraints are required to unambiguously define or solve the geometry of the profile. In other words, you can define a profile by specifying or fixing all the geometry such as orthogonal lines, parallel lines, tangent arcs, and collinear circles in combination with the dimensions (sizes) or locations of such features.

A significant time savings may be realized by using Designer for basic two-dimensional geometric construction. The above profile was not created using the various AutoCAD drawing aids to assure orthogonal lines, tangencies, exact sizes, etc. Rather, it began as a "quick and dirty" sketch, without worrying about exact sizes, locations, connecting endpoints, etc. Designer automatically cleaned up this sketch and applied geometrical constraints based upon the approximate geometry you used to draw the sketch. You then have the option to change these constraints and adding, deleting, or editing dimensions.

Step One: Create a 2-D Sketch

Begin this project by creating a "rough" sketch of the profile you are creating. You may use most of the regular AutoCAD drawing and editing features such as line, circle, arcs, or polylines (although splined polylines are **not** supported). At this point you are not concerned about exact dimensions and locations. The easiest way to draw your sketch is to use an AutoCAD **polyline** (**pline**). If you are unfamiliar with the AutoCAD drawing commands, Chapter 1 discusses how to construct polylines. Use the polyline **line** mode for drawing straight lines and switch to **arc** mode to draw the arc at the top. Although it is not necessary to draw the sketch "exactly," you should try to make it resemble the final shape and size. It should look something like the one shown on page 20. It is not necessary to construct the lines of your sketch in the same order as the one shown here. However, by starting in the lower left-hand corner and working counterclockwise, your numbering scheme will match the one in this tutorial.

If You're New to AutoCAD: Basic Drawing Commands

The AutoCAD *draw* menu has several commands which are used to construct common 2-dimensional entities such as lines, arcs, and circles. When creating a Designer model, the most common drawing commands are: **pline, line, circle**, and **arc**.

The **line** command simply draws a line between two points. You can select **line** from the pull-down menus, or type **line**↵ at the **Command:** prompt. When constructing a line, AutoCAD will prompt you with:

Start point: *You should use the left mouse button to select a point on your drawing for the starting point of the line.*

AutoCAD will then prompt you with:

Endpoint: *Again, use the left mouse button to select the endpoint for the line. Notice that as you drag the mouse around the drawing, AutoCAD will show you a dashed line which indicates the placement of the line.*

Likewise, the **circle** command can either be selected from the **Draw** pull-down menu, or you can simply type **circle↵** at the Command: prompt. AutoCAD will prompt you for the radius of the circle. You can type a numerical value in for the radius, or you can simply drag the mouse and click the left mouse button to select a radius point. You will notice that the circle appears as a dotted line while you are dragging the mouse, until the radius is specified.

The **arc** command is used to draw an arc and can also be selected from the **Draw** pull-down menu, or by typing **arc↵** at the Command: prompt. There are many different ways to specify an arc in AutoCAD and you do not need to be concerned with the different methods here. The default method is a 3-point arc. A 3-point arc requires that you specify a **start point, second point,** and **endpoint**. AutoCAD will prompt you for each of these points and you select the points by clicking the left mouse button. After completing the arc, AutoCAD returns you to the **Command:** prompt.

A **polyline** is a convenient way to draw combinations of straight lines and arcs. A polyline is constructed by entering the command **pline↵** at the command line prompt. You can also create a polyline by using the pull-down menus:

Draw>Polyline>2D

AutoCAD will prompt you with:

Current line width is 0.0000
Arc/Close/Halfwidth/Length/Undo/Width/<Endpoint of line>:

The command enclosed within the <> brackets is always the default command. To use one of the other options you can type the first letter (capitalized) of the command. To create a series of connected straight polylines, simply click the left mouse button in response to the **<Endpoint of line>:** prompt. When the figure is complete, you will type Close or just **C** to complete the set of polylines. If you make a mistake, type Undo, or **U** to undo the previous polyline segment. To create the arc shown in Figure 1-2, type **A** to switch to arc mode. AutoCAD will prompt you with:

<Endpoint of arc>:

You can continue to create connected arcs by clicking the left mouse button in response to this command. Type **L** to switch back to straight line mode. When finished with the polyline, you can return to the **Command:** prompt by typing ↵.

20 Basic 2-D Geometrical Construction

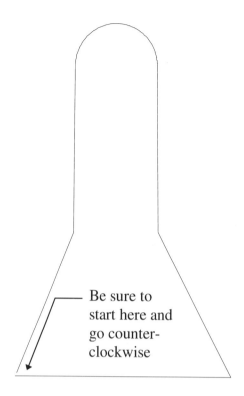

Figure 2-2 *"Rough" sketch of ice scraper*

Step Two: Create a Profile from the Sketch

The **adprofile** command will create a Designer **profile** from your sketch. Designer analyzes the sketch and applies geometrical constraints to "clean it up." Lines are snapped to horizontal or vertical orientations, endpoints are closed, circular features are lined up on the same centerlines, and arcs are snapped tangent to lines. For the best results you should draw your initial "rough" sketch as close to the shape and size expected of the final profile. If the constraints that Designer automatically applies to your sketch are incorrect, you have the option of modifying or deleting any of these constraints. To create a profile:

Select **Designer>Sketch>Profile** *from the pull-down menus.*

Select objects: *Select the entities that are to be included in the profile. You may use the "Window" feature of AutoCAD to select all. If your sketch was drawn with an AutoCAD polyline, you need only select one portion of the polyline and the entire sketch will be activated.*

Press ↵ to complete the selection.

Designer will display the following message:

```
Solved underconstrained sketch requiring 6 dimensions /
constraints
```

You should see the rough sketch "cleaned up" by Designer as it applies geometric constraints. Endpoints are closed, lines that were drawn "close" to horizontal and vertical are re-oriented to appropriate orthogonality, etc.

Constraints and Dimensions

The sketch is now a profile with geometric constraints but no dimensions. After executing the **adprofile** command, Designer will indicate how many constraints are needed to fully define the profile. This message means that you must specify six other geometric constraints **or** dimensions before the ice scraper profile is fully defined.

Designer automatically applies constraints when you execute the **adprofile** command. Your sketch is analyzed and rules are applied to snap lines to the vertical and horizontal positions, close endpoints, and make arcs tangent to connecting lines. The geometric constraints may be modified before you apply parametric dimensions (numeric constraints). Geometric constraints and numeric constraints (parametric dimensions) are both required to fully define a profile. You can remove geometric constraints (such as a "vertical" constraint on a line) and then define the geometry by adding more dimensions. If you add geometric constraints (such as specifying that two lines must be parallel), then Designer will require fewer dimensions to fully define the profile.

You add the dimensions after the geometry has been defined. Sometimes, the geometric constraints contradict the dimensions you are trying to apply to the model. For example, if you are dimensioning an angle between two lines and the lines have previously been constrained to be perpendicular to each other, the angular dimension may only be 90 degrees. If the perpendicular constraint is removed, then the angle between the lines can then be dimensioned to a value other than 90°. In Chapter 3, you will experiment with adding, modifying, and deleting geometric constraints on this profile.

Showing constraints

Before adding dimensions to the profile, it is sometimes useful to view or examine the geometric constraints that Designer applied to the sketch. The **adshowcon** command can be used to show the constraints on the 2-D geometry.

Select: **Designer>Sketch>Constraints>Show**

All/Select/Next/(exit): *Type A to show **all** of the constraints defining the sketch. As an alternative, you can select a specific feature and show only the constraints applied to that feature. For complicated geometry, showing individual features is preferred.*

Press ↵ to complete the selection.

22 Basic 2-D Geometrical Construction

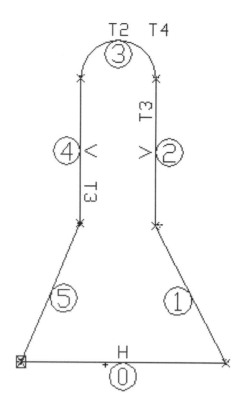

Figure 2-3 *Geometric constraints viewed with the **adshowcon** command*

Your sketch should look like the one shown in Figure 2-3. The symbols T, H, and V are used by Designer to identify the geometric constraints applied to your sketch. The numbers associated with the symbol refer to the entity, which is indicated by the circled numbers.

Constraint type --------- C3 ------- Partner entity number

③ ---- Entity number

Horizontal: (Hor) Horizontal lines are parallel to the X-axis. (**H symbol**)

Vertical: (Ver) Vertical lines are parallel to the Y-axis. (**V symbol**)

Perpendicular: (PErp) Perpendicular lines have slopes 90 degrees from each other. (**L symbol**)

Parallel: (PAr) Parallel lines have the same slope and orientation. (**P symbol**)

Tangent: (Tan) The slope of two entities is identical at the point where they meet. Allowable pairs are two Arcs or Circles or one Line and an Arc or a Circle. (**T symbol**)

Collinear: (CL) Entities fall on the same line. (**C symbol**)

Concentric: (CN) Concentric Arcs and Circles have coincident center points. (**N symbol**)

Projected: (PRoj) The selected point of an entity joins the unbounded definition of a second entity. (A projected constraint does not show a symbol.) When you apply a projected constraint between an Arc or Circle center and another item, you must use the Center mode of the **AutoCAD OSNAP** command before you select the Arc or Circle.

Join: (Join) The selected endpoints are coincident. Use this option to close a gap between geometry in your sketch set. (A joined constraint does not show a symbol.)

Xvalue: The center points of Circles have the same X coordinates. (**X symbol**)

Yvalue: The center points of Circles have the same Y coordinates. (**Y symbol**)

Radius: Arcs and Circles have the same radius. You can apply this constraint only after you have dimensioned one or more radii for Arcs or Circles. (**R symbol**)

In Figure 2-3, notice that the arc has two geometric constraints, T2 and T4. This means that the arc is tangent to both line 2 and line 4. The **H** and **V** symbols mean that lines 4, 2, and 0 are constrained to be **H**orizontal and **V**ertical respectively. The remaining lines, 1 and 5, do not have any geometric constraints assigned, so dimensional or numeric constraints must be added to define the geometry of these lines.

How does Designer apply constraints?

When you execute the **adprofile** command, Designer analyzes your sketch and applies geometric constraints based upon how "closely" you drew certain features to ideal. The **angular tolerance** determines how many degrees away from horizontal and vertical a line must be in order for Designer to "clean up" the line and make it exactly horizontal or vertical. You can control the angular tolerance by using the **Designer>Settings** pull-down menu to open the **adsettings** dialogue box. The reference section of this book will give you more information about the settings that Designer uses to constrain a sketch.

At this point, it is helpful to understand the types of constraints Designer applies. Consider the following sketch and the resulting "constrained" profile, which is shown in Figure 2-5.

24 Basic 2-D Geometrical Construction

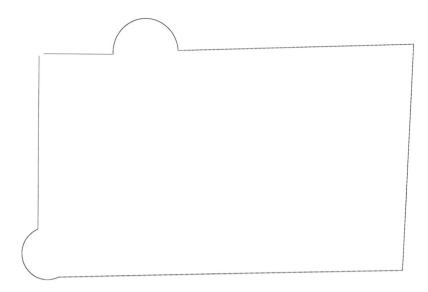

Figure 2-4 *Unconstrained sketch*

Notice that the lines in this sketch are not parallel, perpendicular, vertical, or horizontal. The arcs are not tangent to the lines and some of the lines that should be collinear are not. Figure 2-5 shows the same sketch after Designer applied constraints. The **adshowcon** command was used to show the constraints which were applied by Designer. In particular:

- Lines 1 and 3 were sketched close to vertical, so Designer applied vertical constraints.
- Lines 0, 2, and 6 were sketched nearly horizontal, so Designer applied horizontal constraints.
- Lines 2 and 6 were sketched to lie nearly on the same line, so Designer applied a collinear constraint to these lines.
- Arc 5 was sketched nearly tangent to lines 0 and 3, so Designer applied a tangent constraint to this arc and these lines.

In addition to these constraints, Designer would have applied parallel constraints to lines that were nearly parallel. If two arcs or circles were sketched close to coincident, Designer would have applied a concentric constraint to those entities. If you do not like the constraints that Designer applies automatically when executing the **adprofile** command, you have the choice of deleting constraints, modifying, or adding constraints to your profile. Chapter 3 will cover how to modify and delete constraints.

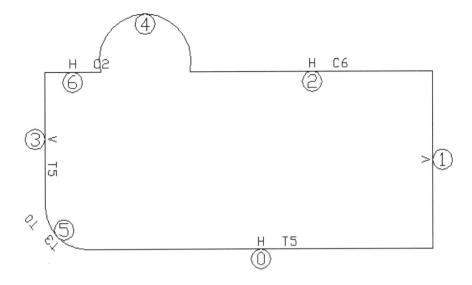

Figure 2-5 *Designer profile after constraints have been added*

Table 2-1 summarizes the ten different types of geometric constraints and associated symbols used by Designer.

Table 2-1 *Designer Geometric Constraints*

Symbol	Constraint
H	entity is horizontal
V	entity is vertical
L	entities are perpendicular to each other
P	entities are parallel to each other
T	entity is tangent to circle or arc
C	collinear entities fall on the same line
N	arcs or circles have the same centerpoint
X	entities have the same X value
Y	entities have the same Y value
R	circular entities have the same radius values

Adding dimensions

The **adpardim** command is used to add parametric dimensions (numeric constraints) to the profile. There is a fundamental difference between parametric dimensions and regular AutoCAD dimensions. AutoCAD dimensions give a numeric value, or a measure of the size of a particular piece of the geometry. AutoCAD dimensions do not define or drive the geometry of the model; they only indicate the size or location. On the other hand, parametric dimensions actually define or drive the geometry of the model. As you define a parametric dimension, the model geometry will be updated to reflect the new value for this dimension. Parametric dimensions are always added after the geometric constraints are defined by Designer when creating the profile from the rough sketch. To define or add a parametric dimension to your model, you type **adpardim** at the command line or use the pull-down menu:

Select: **Designer>Sketch>Add Dimension**

Various types of dimensions or numeric constraints may be added to the sketch. The type of dimension is assigned according to the context of the entity. For example, a horizontal or vertically constrained line can only be assigned horizontal or vertical dimensions. Lines at some other angle, such as lines 1 and 5 above, can be assigned either aligned, vertical, or horizontal dimensions. When adding dimensions to these lines you will be prompted for the dimension type. Circular features are dimensioned as diameters or as radii depending upon the context of the feature.

Relative or absolute dimensions

When assigning dimensions you can select a single entity and specify the size of that entity. Alternatively, you can select two separate entities and specify the distance or angle between those entities. The parametric dimensioning is context sensitive, so the type of dimension depends upon both how the entity is selected and the location of the selection point on the entity. Designer will prompt you to select an entity. Upon selecting the first entity, you then have the choice of selecting a second entity, or selecting the location of the dimension placement. If you select two entities, such as adjoining lines, you can specify either an angle between these lines, or a distance apart for the lines. The cursor location used to select the lines will determine whether they are dimensioned as a distance or as an angle between the lines. If you select a circular feature followed by a line, then Designer will expect you to place a dimension locating the distance of the centerpoint away from the line. If you simply select the circular feature and then locate the dimension, Designer will expect the diameter of that feature.

Linear dimensions

Select first item: *Choose the midpoint of one of the lines to dimension.*

You will then be prompted for the value of the dimension (the current value is indicated inside the < > brackets). If you type the ↵ key in response to this value, then the dimension you used to draw the sketch will be accepted as the parametric dimension used to define the profile. Normally, you do not want to accept the same value for the dimension as you used to construct the sketch.

Dimension types

You may specify four different types of linear dimensions when selecting a line. The options are:

Undo/Hor/Ver/Align/Par/Dimension value <#>:

Horizontal (Hor): Creates a horizontal dimension. Indicates the horizontal length of the line.

Vertical (Ver): Creates a vertical dimension. Indicates the vertical length of the line.

Aligned (Align): The actual length of the line is given, parallel to the direction of the line.

Parallel (Par): The distance between two parallel lines is indicated. Two lines or points must be picked.

When selecting two lines, be sure to select near the appropriate endpoints to specify a linear dimension. If you select the lines near the midpoint, Designer will apply an angular dimension between the lines. For example, selecting the angle at the "x" location will allow you to specify a linear dimension:

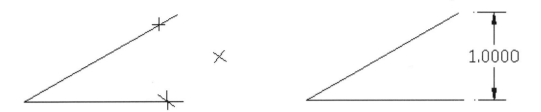

Figure 2-6 *Dimensioning angular distance*

Angular dimensions

Select first item: *Select the midpoint of one of the lines enclosing the angle and then repeat with the other line.*

Select second item or place dimension: *Select the midpoint of the other line.*

Specify dimension placement: *For angular dimension, select angle between the lines.*

Undo/Dimension value (#): *You may change the angle by typing in a new one.*

Since the dimension type depends upon the location used to select the lines, be sure to select near the midpoint of the lines. Designer will then place an angular measurement between the lines. For example, the same angle is selected near the endpoint at the "x"s and you are allowed to input an angular dimension:

Figure 2-7 *Dimensioning an angle*

Step Three: Add Dimensions to the Sketch

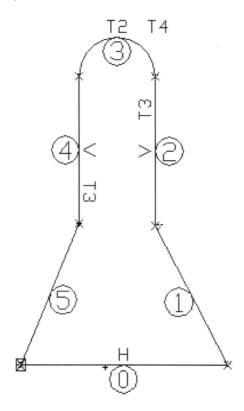

Figure 2-8 *Profile of ice scraper*

After you've completed the sketch shown in Figure 2-2, use the **adpardim** command to add dimensions (numeric constraints). Select each line or arc separately and type in the value for the linear dimension for that item. When specifying the linear dimension for the line, you will first select the line near the midpoint, and then select an area outside the line that will locate the dimension placement. When dimensioning angles between the lines, you will select the first line near the midpoint, followed by the second line near the midpoint, and finally the dimension placement is between the two lines. As you add dimensions, Designer will automatically modify the geometry in response to the new values. Designer will tell you how many dimensions or constraints are needed to fully solve the sketch. Each time you add a dimension this number will decrease until Designer has solved the fully constrained sketch. As you apply dimensions to the sketch, certain features will be highlighted (shown as dashed lines). The highlighting indicates that those features have not yet been defined geometrically. These features will change to solid lines as the geometry is defined.

Select: **Designer>Sketch>Add Dimension**

Select first item: *Pick near the midpoint of line 4.*

Select second item or place dimension: *Place dimension to the left of the line.*

Undo/Hor/Ver/Align/Par/Dimension value <current>: *3↵*

Solved under constrained sketch requiring 5 dimensions / constraints (*Notice that Designer will always update this message as a dimension or constraint is added to the sketch. The number of required dimensions will decrement each time until the sketch is fully solved*)

Select first item: *Pick line 5.*

Select second item or place dimension: *Place dimension to the left of the line.*

Undo/Hor/Ver/Align/Par/Dimension value <current>: *align*

Undo/Hor/Ver/Align/Par/Dimension value <current>: *3↵*

Solved under constrained sketch requiring 4 dimensions / constraints

Select first item: *Pick near the midpoint of line 5.*

Select second item or place dimension: *Pick near the midpoint of line 0.*

Specify dimension placement: *Place between the lines.*

Undo/Dimension value<90>: *65*

Solved under constrained sketch requiring 3 dimensions / constraints

Select first item: *Pick near the midpoint of line 0.*

Select second item or place dimension: *Place dimension below the line.*

Undo/Hor/Ver/Align/Par/Dimension value <current>: *4↵*

Solved under constrained sketch requiring 2 dimensions / constraints

Select first item: *Pick near the midpoint of line 0.*

Select second item or place dimension: *Pick line 1.*

Specify dimension placement: *Place between the lines.*

Undo/Dimension value<57>: *65*

Solved under constrained sketch requiring 1 dimensions / constraints

Select first item: *Pick near the midpoint of line 2.*

Select second item or place dimension: *Place dimension to the right of the line.*

30 Basic 2-D Geometrical Construction

Undo/Hor/Ver/Align/Par/Dimension value <current>: *3*↵

Solved fully constrained sketch

When you've specified enough dimensions to completely define the geometry, Designer will let you know that the sketch is fully defined. This means that all of the geometry is completely defined. Your sketch should look like Figure 2-9.

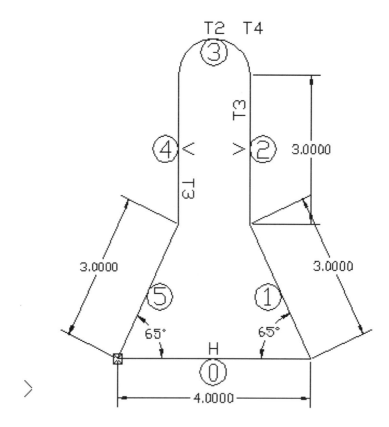

Figure 2-9 *Completed 2-D dimensioned and constrained profile*

After completing this exercise, be sure to save your drawing file as *scraper.dwg*. You will use this drawing as the basis for later exercises in Chapters 3 and 4.

If You're New to AutoCAD: Saving Drawing Files

You can save your work in a file for later use by using the **save** command. You can select this command from the **File** pull-down menu, or you can simply type **save**↵ at the **Command:** prompt. You will see the **File** dialogue box and can specify a disk drive (floppy or hard) and a corresponding directory in which to save your work. Type a filename (must be less than 8 alphanumeric characters) in the file box. AutoCAD will automatically append a **.dwg** extension to the filename.

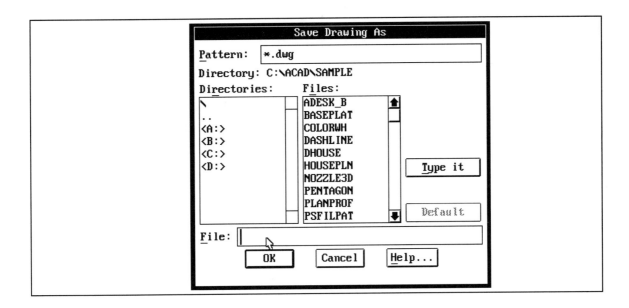

End of Chapter Summary

Your completed two-dimensional profile should look like the one shown in Figure 2-9. This profile is a fully dimensioned and constrained representation of the ice scraper. You did not use any of the conventional drawing aids to create the geometry, but allowed Designer to automatically clean up a rough sketch. Using Designer, you can now easily modify and edit this geometry. In the next lesson you will investigate the relationships between parametric dimensions and geometric constraints. Designer's parametric editing capabilities will be exploited to modify the geometry of this ice scraper profile.

32 Basic 2-D Geometrical Construction

Exercises

Create the following profiles using Designer. Construct a profile of the object shown below according to the dimensions given. Start by creating a sketch, generating a profile (**adprofile** command), and finally adding parametric dimensions.

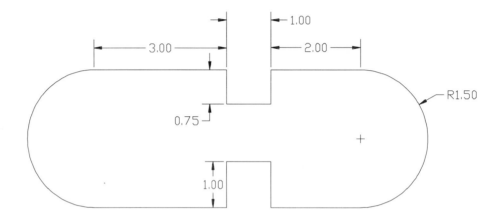

Ex 2-1

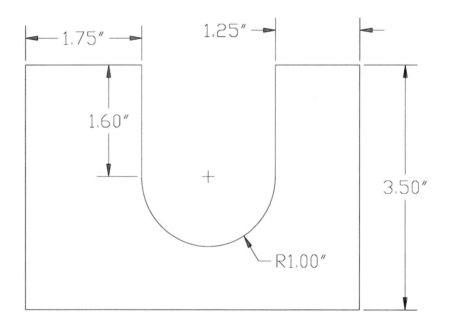

Ex 2-2

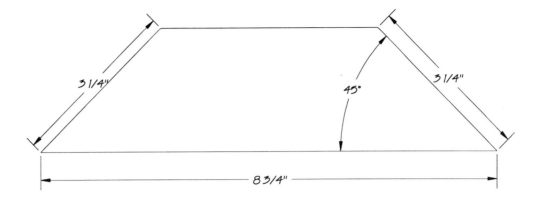

Ex 2-3

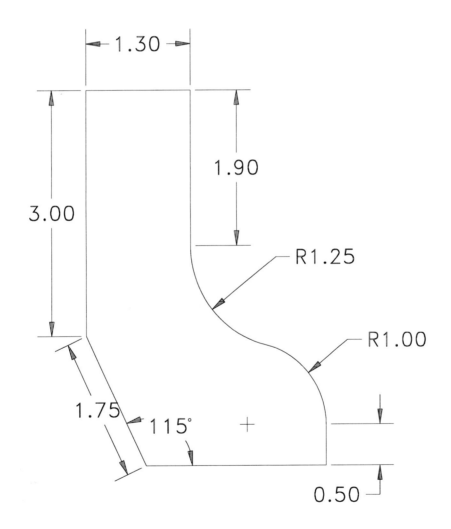

Ex 2-4

34 Basic 2-D Geometrical Construction

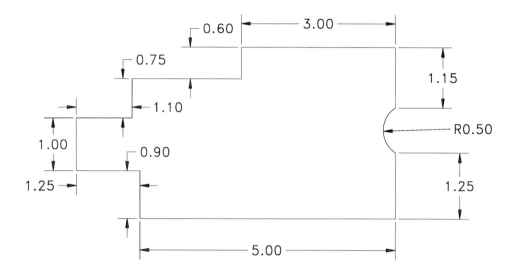

Ex 2-5

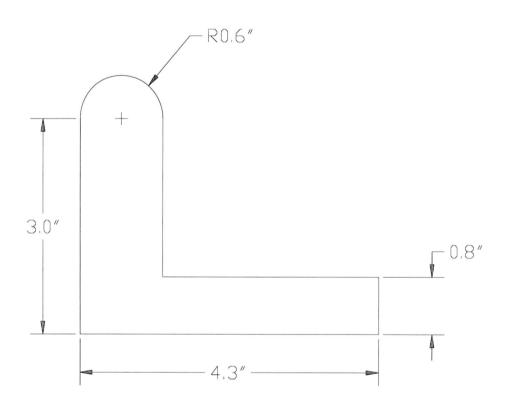

Ex 2-6

Exercises **35**

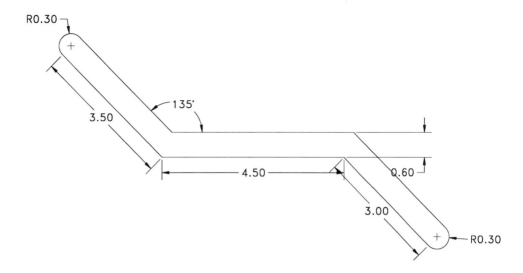

Ex 2-7

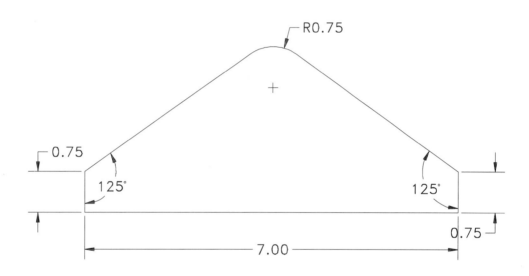

Ex 2-8

Chapter 3

Understanding Constraints and Construction Geometry

When you have completed this lesson you will:

1. **Understand how Designer constrains a sketch**
2. **Understand the relationship between geometric constraints and dimensions**
3. **Be able to add, delete, and modify geometric constraints**
4. **Be able to use construction geometry**

Introduction

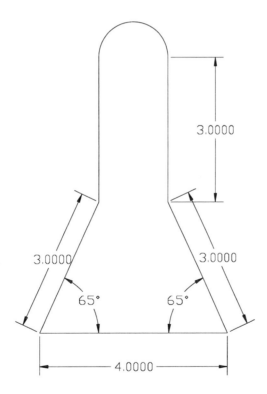

Figure 3-1 *Fully dimensioned ice scraper profile*

In the previous chapter you used Designer's 2-D profile features to create this profile of an ice scraper. You started with a rough sketch and Designer automatically cleaned up your sketch and applied geometric constraints. You finished defining the profile by adding any necessary parametric dimensions. This lesson will begin with the basic profile you created in Chapter 2. You will explore the relationship between geometric constraints and parametric dimensions by editing the constraints that were automatically applied by Designer. As constraints are deleted or changed, the number and type of dimensions required to define the geometry changes by a corresponding amount. Since constraints and parametric dimensions are the foundation of Designer it is important that you have a good understanding of these concepts. The simple ice scraper profile will be used to illustrate the relationships between these important concepts.

This chapter will also introduce you to the technique of using construction geometry. Construction geometry is using additional lines, arcs, or circles as frames of reference for constraining the profile geometry of your sketch. Construction geometry is not a part of the profile and is ignored by Designer when creating 3-D models from the 2-D profile. For certain type of profiles, construction geometry is a powerful technique to assist you in defining the profile geometry. To illustrate the concept of construction geometry, you will re-create the profile of the ice scraper in this chapter using construction geometry.

Relationships Between Constraints and Dimensions

As discussed in Chapter 2, Designer will analyze your sketch and logically apply geometric constraints according to the way in which you drew the sketch. Initially, Designer does not add parametric dimensions to the geometry of the sketch; you must do this yourself after the geometric constraints have been applied. After executing the **adprofile** command, Designer will report the number of constraints and/or dimensions needed to fully define the geometry. You have the option of adding either constraints or dimensions to the sketch until its geometry is fully and unambiguously defined. As constraints/dimensions are added to the profile, Designer updates the status of the geometry and reports the number of constraints/dimensions required to completely define the geometry.

You are not required to have the geometry fully constrained before you can use the profile for other Designer operations. However, it is desirable to have the profile fully defined before extruding it or using it in any 3-D model. Fully constrained sketches behave predictably when dimension values are modified. Fully constrained sketches are completely and unambiguously defined, so they can be used as a basis for manufacturing the part.

Underconstrained Sketch

If the sketch does not contain enough information to define its size and shape completely, Designer will report that it is underconstrained. The dimensions that Designer uses to define the geometry are the dimensions you used when you initially drew the sketch. Until you explicitly define or change those dimensions, Designer will report an underconstrained sketch. As you add dimensions and/or constraints Designer continues to report the number required to finish defining its geometry.

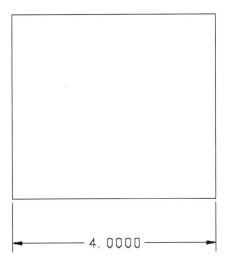

Figure 3-2 *Underconstrained sketch. Vertical distance needs to be specified.*

Overconstrained Sketch

If one or more features of the sketch are dimensioned twice, or if the dimensioning is geometrically inconsistent, Designer will report that the sketch is overconstrained. You need to remove either a dimension or a geometric constraint to solve this problem. For example, Figure 3-3 shows an overconstrained sketch. Because the sketch is orthogonal, you do not need to specify both the radius of the arc and the horizontal distance. The geometric constraints require that if one of these dimensions is given then the other one is unnecessary. If your sketch is complex, it may not be readily apparent why it is overconstrained. The **adshowcon** command (discussed below) may be useful to help you understand why the sketch is overconstrained.

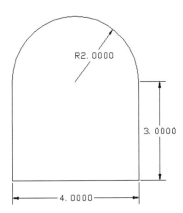

Figure 3-3 *Overconstrained sketch. Both radius and horizontal distance are specified.*

Viewing, Deleting, and Changing Constraints

Occasionally Designer will apply constraint rules that are not what you expect, or that are too confining for the model you are trying to create. Sometimes, Designer will report an overconstrained sketch as you add dimensions. For these cases, it is useful to view the

40 Understanding Constraints and Construction Geometry

constraints that are used to define your profile. You then have the capability to delete, add, or modify any constraints defining your model. The tutorial described in this chapter will show you how to delete and modify constraints and parametric dimensions. As you increase the number of geometric constraints in your sketch, you decrease the number of required dimensions needed to completely define the profile.

To illustrate the relationship between geometric and numeric constraints, we will use the original profile you created in Chapter 2 of the ice scraper. Open the file, *scraper.dwg* or the file you saved at the completion of Chapter 2. The two-dimensional profile should look like the one shown in Figure 3-1.

If You're New to AutoCAD: Opening Drawing Files

To open an existing drawing, you use the **open** command. This command can also be selected from the **File** pull-down menu or can be typed at the **Command:** prompt. Use the mouse to select the appropriate directory or disk drive. The **Open Drawing** dialogue box will give you a list of all drawing files on the current directory. You can select a file by highlighting it and double clicking with the left mouse button or the name can by typed in the **Files:** box.

Execute the **adshowcon** command to show the constraints that are active in your sketch.

Select: **Designer>Sketch>Constraints>Show**

Type **A** to show All constraints.

Press ↵ to complete the selection.

Your sketch should look like the one below in Figure 3-4. The **H** symbol denotes a horizontal constraint for that entity, the **V** symbol denotes a vertical constraint, and the **T** symbol specifies an arc that is constrained tangent to a line.

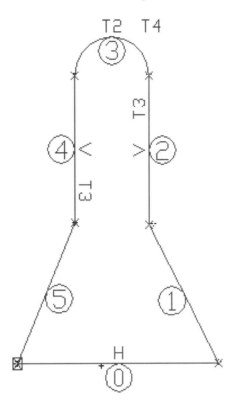

Figure 3-4 *Constraints that were applied automatically by Designer*

Adding constraints

In the previous chapter, you saw how the geometry could be modified by adding or changing parametric dimensions. You can also modify the geometry by adding or changing the geometric constraints applied to the sketch. To illustrate this concept, you will add a **perpendicular** constraint between lines 5 and 0, shown above. The **adaddcon** command will be used to add a perpendicular constraint between these lines. However, before you can add a perpendicular constraint, the 65° angle between these lines must be removed. To remove a parametric dimension in Designer, you simply erase the value with the AutoCAD **erase** command.

If You're New to AutoCAD: Erasing in AutoCAD

The **erase** command is used to delete complete objects, individual entities, or complete drawings. To use this command you must select the object(s) that you want to erase. AutoCAD allows you to first select the entities and then execute the command (noun-verb), or you can execute the **erase** command and then select the entities (verb-noun). You have the option of

> selecting entities individually by simply clicking the left mouse button on an object, or you can draw a **window** to select all the objects contained within that window.
>
> To select objects within a window, click the left mouse button to locate one corner of the window. Drag the mouse and you will drag out a rectangle on the screen. To complete the window selection, click the mouse again to define the other corner.
>
> At the **Command:** prompt, type **erase** (or **e** for short) ↵
>
> To complete the **erase** operation, press ↵ again to return to the **Command:** prompt.

At the **Command:** prompt, type **erase** (or **e** for short) ↵

Select any location on the 65° dimension to erase it.

Since you've erased one of the parametric dimensions that was used to define the profile, Designer now reports that the underconstrained sketch needs one constraint/dimension to be solved.

You are now ready to add a perpendicular constraint between lines 0 and 5. Constraints can be added to a profile with the **adaddcon** command. Type the command:

Select: **Designer>Sketch>Constraints>Add.**↵

You are given the choice of ten different types of geometric constraints to be added to a feature on the sketch.

Hor/Ver/PErp/PAr/Tan/CL/CN/PRoj/Join/XValue/Yvalue/Radius/(exit): **PE**↵ *Select a perpendicular constraint.*

Select line: *Pick near the midpoint of line 5.*

Select line: *Pick near the midpoint of line 0.*

Press ↵ to complete the selection. Designer will "snap" line 5 vertical so that it is perpendicular to line 0.

To see the new constraints applied to your sketch, execute the **adshowcon** command:

command: adshowcon↵

Type **A** to show All constraints.

Press ↵ to complete the selection.

Your sketch should look like the one shown on page 43. Notice that the symbols **L0** and **L5** have been added. The Designer symbol **L0** denotes that line 5 is perpendicular to line 0, and the symbol **L5** denotes that line 0 is perpendicular to line 5.

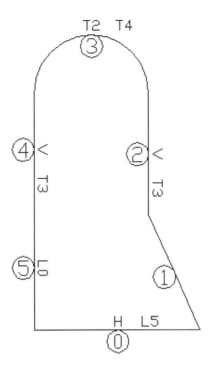

Figure 3-5 *Ice scraper profile with "perpendicular" constraint added*

Removing constraints

You may find that as you add a dimension Designer gives you the following message:

```
Highlighted items and dimensions form an overconstrained
system.  Remove a highlighted dim or a constraint.
(Enter) to continue:
```

This message indicates that you have a geometric constraint and a dimension value that contradict each other, or that a feature has been dimensioned more than once. One of the constraints or a dimension must be removed.

The **addelcon** command is used to remove a constraint. You will be prompted to select a constraint to remove upon executing this command. Select the constraint you wish to remove. Designer will then remove that constraint and you may continue adding dimensions.

Since we want to get our sketch back to the original shape before adding the perpendicular constraint, we will use this command and select line 5 in order to remove the perpendicular constraint (L0 or L5).

Select: **Designer>Sketch>Constraints>Delete**↵

All/Select item to edit: *Pick line 5.*

Select constraint to remove: *Pick one of the L symbols to remove the perpendicular constraint.*

Select line: ↵ to complete the selection.

You may now repeat the **adpardim** command to get the profile back to its original shape and size. Dimension the angle between lines 0 and 5 back to the original 65° as you did in Chapter 2.

Changing dimensions

A parametric CAD system creates a complete geometrical model of your design. Therefore, if you change a single dimension on the drawing, all related geometry will be automatically updated to reflect these changes. For example, if you specify the centerpoint of a hole to be a certain distance from the edge of a part, the centerpoint moves if the edge is moved when editing the drawing.

To illustrate, we will increase the length of the ice scraper handle from 3.0 units to 4.0 units. Dimensions can be modified by the **admoddim** command.

Select: **Designer>Change Dimension**↵

Select dimension to change: *Choose the 3.0000 vertical dimension on the handle.*

New value for dimension <#>: *Enter new value for dimension,* **4.0**↵

Since you have just edited a completely defined solid model (rather than a drawing), all related geometry will be automatically updated to reflect the new value for the dimension. The handle length should increase to 4.0, so your ice scraper profile looks like the one shown in Figure 3-6.

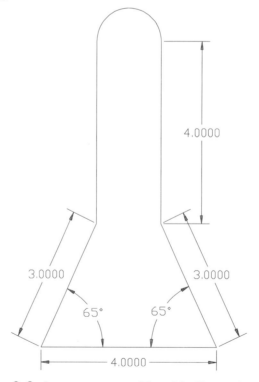

Figure 3-6 *Ice scraper profile with dimension edited*

Using Different Combinations of Constraints and Dimensions to Define a Profile

Your objective in adding dimensions to a sketch is to completely define the size and location of every element of that sketch. In this simple ice scraper example, we defined the profile by dimensioning the two 65° angles and the other lengths shown in Figure 3-6. However, there are many other combinations of dimensions that will define the same size and geometry. For example, you could dimension the other features in this profile using just horizontal and vertical distances without needing to define those angles.

To illustrate how you can use alternate methods of dimensioning, you will delete the two angular dimensions and redefine them using other features.

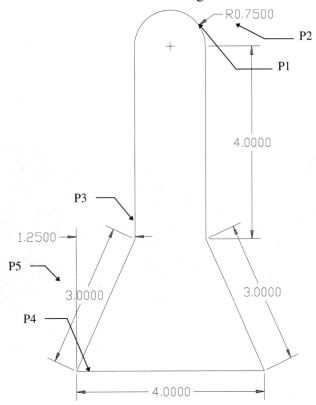

Figure 3-7 *Modifying the geometry by changing constraints and dimensions*

Erase the two angular dimensions.

Command: erase *(select each of the 65° dimensions with the mouse)* ↵ *to complete the selection*

Select: **Designer>Sketch>Add dimension**

Select first item: *Pick P1, any location on the radius of the upper arc.*

Select second item or place dimension: *Place dimension to the right of the arc (point P2).*

Undo/Dimension value<current>: **.75**

Solved under constrained sketch requiring 1 dimensions/constraints *This assigns the radius of the upper arc a value of 0.75.*

Select first item: *Pick **P3**, towards the lower end of the vertical line.*

Select second item or place dimension: *Pick P4, the left end of the lower horizontal line.*

Undo/Hor/Ver/Align/Par/Dimension value <current>: **hor**

Undo/Hor/Ver/Align/Par/Dimension value <current>: **1.25↵**

Solved fully constrained sketch

Press ↵ to complete the profile.

Your profile should look like the one shown in Figure 3-7. Notice that the geometry is slightly different than what you originally specified with the 65° angles. For this particular problem, it is probably easier to dimension the geometry using equal 65° angles rather than trying to find the horizontal location of the two lines representing the handle. As you gain experience using Designer, you'll be able to look at a sketch and decide which combination of dimensions are the easiest to specify to completely define the profile.

Using Construction Geometry

Designer allows you to use **construction geometry** to assist in constraining a sketch and controlling the sketch geometry. **Construction geometry** is any line, arc, or circle that is included as part of the sketch profile and is a linetype other than the linetype of the sketch. Figure 3-8 shows an example of construction geometry. The 40° diagonal line is a hidden linetype and is used as an aide in defining the slope of the "steps" in the profile shown on page 47. When used properly, construction geometry can greatly reduce the number of constraints and dimensions needed to define a profile, and also give you greater control over the sketch geometry. The diagonal construction line shown in Figure 3-8 allows you to define the slope of the steps by a single dimension, the angle of the line with respect to the horizontal. The endpoints of the steps are constrained by Designer to be attached to the construction line. Without construction geometry, you would need to carefully define each horizontal and vertical dimension for the steps in order to define the slope. Any time you have geometry that lies on a radius, in a straight line, or at an angle to other geometry, you can greatly simplify the profile definition by taking advantage of construction geometry. Because the construction geometry linetype (hidden or phantom) is different from the sketch linetype (continuous), Designer ignores the construction geometry when performing 3-D operations.

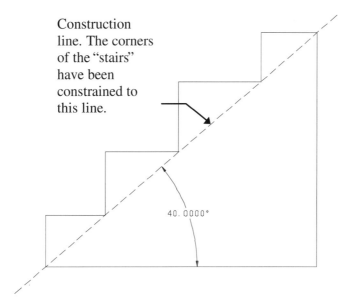

Figure 3-8 *Using a "construction line" to define profile geometry*

Using Construction Geometry to Define the Ice Scraper Profile

To illustrate the application of construction geometry, you will redraw the sketch of the ice scraper profile. The sides of the blade will be constrained tangent to a construction circle instead of using two 65° angles to define the blades. A horizontal construction line will be used to orient the endpoints of the handle and blades in the same horizontal line.

If You're New to AutoCAD: Changing Linetypes

There are several ways to change linetypes in AutoCAD. Designer uses a default linetype of **continuous**. When creating construction geometry, the default linetype will need to be changed to **hidden**. The easiest way to change a linetype in Designer is to type the **chprop** (change property) command at the **Command:** prompt, or to use the **Modify>Entity...** pull-down menu.

To use the **chprop** command, simply type **chprop**↵ at the **Command:** prompt. AutoCAD will prompt you to:

Select objects: *Using the left mouse button, select any lines you want to change and press ↵ when finished.*

AutoCAD will respond with:

Change what property (Color/Elev/LAyer/LType/Thickness)?: *Type* **LT**↵ *to change the linetype.*

New linetype <continuous>: *Type* **hidden**↵ *to change the linetype to a "hidden" line. Note that the current linetype is displayed in the < > brackets. To complete this operation, press ↵ again. You should see the selected linetype become "hidden."*

48 Understanding Constraints and Construction Geometry

Another way to modify the line type is to use the **Modify Entity** graphical dialogue box. From the pull-down menus select:

Modify>Entity...

You will be prompted to select an entity. Use the left mouse button to select the line you wish to change. The **Modify Line** dialogue box will appear.

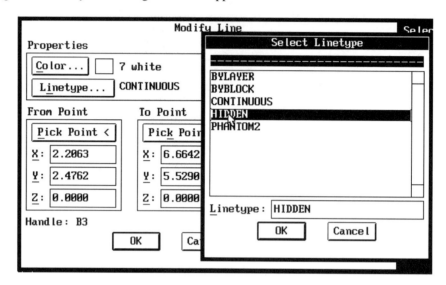

Using the mouse, select the **Linetype** box and the **Select Linetype** dialogue box will appear. Click on **hidden** linetype and then on the **OK** button when finished.

1. Using an AutoCAD polyline or lines, draw the sketch of the ice scraper profile shown in Figure 3-9.

2. Use an AutoCAD circle to draw the construction circle shown in Figure 3-9.

3. Draw a horizontal construction line like the one shown in Figure 3-9.

4. Use the AutoCAD **chprop** command to change the linetypes of the construction circle and line to **hidden** linetypes.

5. Use the Designer **adprofile** command to create a profile from this sketch. Be sure to select both the ice scraper profile and the construction geometry when prompted to select items.

Using Construction Geometry 49

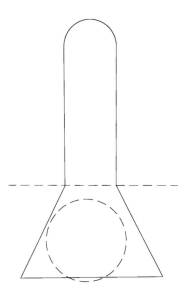

Figure 3-9 *Ice scraper sketch with construction circle and construction line added*

Verify the constraints that Designer applied to your sketch. The construction line should have a **horizontal** (H) constraint applied. If you draw the circle close enough to the ice scraper blade, Designer may have added a **tangent** (T) constraint between the blade and the circle. Use the **adshowcon** command to show all the constraints. Your profile should look similar to the one shown in Figure 3-10.

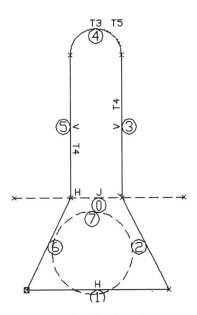

Figure 3-10 *Ice scraper sketch showing geometric constraints*

The next step is to define the dimensions and add any constraints required to attach the sketch profile geometry to the construction geometry.

Use the Designer **adpardim** command to add dimensions to the profile. Add the linear dimensions shown in Figure 3-11.

50 Using Different Combinations of Constraints and Dimensions to Define a Profile

The next step is to constrain the three sides of the ice scraper blade as tangent to the circle and finally to define the diameter of the circle. Use the Designer **adadcon** command to add these constraints. Type the command or use the pull-down menus:

Select: **Designer>Sketch>Constraints>Add.↵**

You are given the choice of ten different types of geometric constraints to be added to a feature on the sketch.

Hor/Ver/PErp/PAr/Tan/CL/CN/PRoj/Join/XValue/Yvalue/Radius/(exit): **T↵** *(select a tangent constraint)*

Select line: *Pick the circle.*

Select line: *Pick one of the three lines defining the blade.↵*

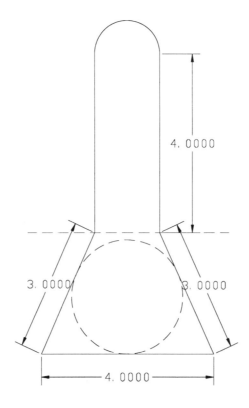

Figure 3-11 *Ice scraper profile with tangent constraints applied between circle and blade*

Repeat this command until all three lines have been constrained as tangent to the circle. Since you previously defined the length of these lines, the angles between the sides of the blade will always be equal. You have now to define only the diameter of the circle, and you have a fully defined profile.

Use the **adpardim** command to give the circle a radius of 2.5.

Your ice scraper profile should look like the one shown in Figure 3-12. If you need to change the angle of the blade, you can simply edit the radius of the construction circle, and the blade angles will be automatically adjusted.

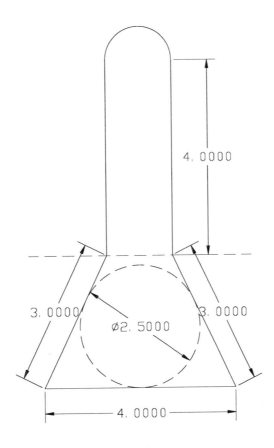

Figure 3-12 *Fully defined ice scraper profile using construction geometry*

End of Chapter Summary

You've taken the fully dimensioned and constrained representation of the ice scraper and modified the dimensions and constraints. With Designer, there are multiple ways to define a 2-D profile, and some are easier than others. You can define the profile through various combinations of geometric constraints and parametric dimensions. As you add constraints, you need fewer dimensions to define the geometry. In cases where the profile geometry falls on a line or coincides with a circle, you can greatly simplify the profile definition by using construction geometry as a drawing aide. In the next lesson we will use this profile to create a three-dimensional solid model of the ice scraper.

Exercises

For the following problems, use Designer to start with the sketch similar to the one shown on the left side, and create the fully constrained profile shown on the right side.

52 Understanding Constraints and Construction Geometry

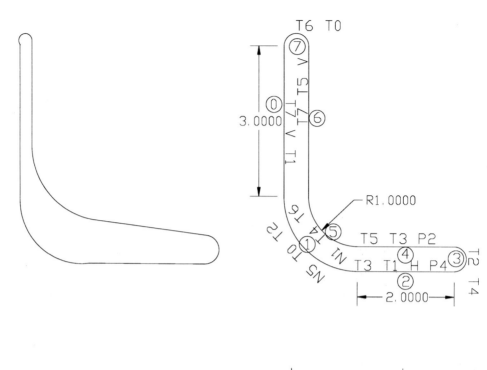

Ex 3-1

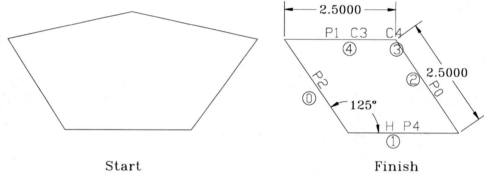

Start   Finish

Ex 3-2

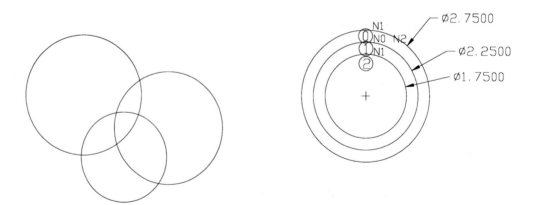

Ex 3-3

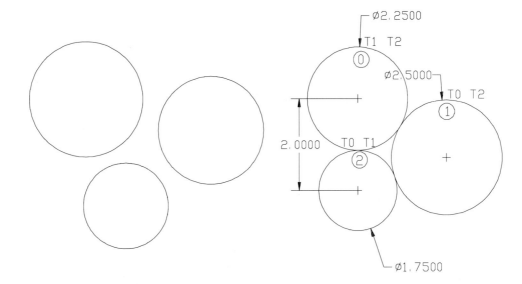

Ex 3-4

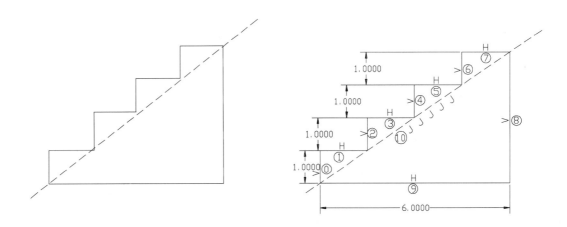

Ex 3-5

Chapter 4

Creating a 3-D Solid Model from a 2-D Profile

When you have completed this lesson you will:

1. Understand how to extrude a 2-dimensional profile to create a 3-dimensional solid model
2. Be able to add 3-D features to the solid model, such as holes, chamfers, and fillets
3. Understand how easy it is to edit and modify a 3-D Designer model

Introduction

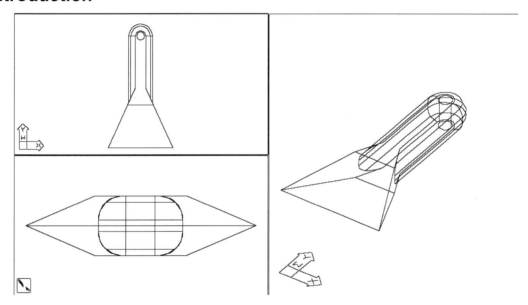

Figure 4-1 *Complete 3-D solid model of "ice scraper"*

In this lesson you will take the two-dimensional profile generated in Chapter 2 and apply the Designer Extrude command to create the 3-D solid model shown in Figure 4-1. Designer can add special features to your solid model such as holes, countersinks, counterbores, fillets, and chamfers. These features will be added to the basic 3-D model to create a chamfered blade, filleted handle, and the hole in the handle.

The model you create will be a **parametric** representation of the physical object. A parameter is a physical property that determines the behavior of the model. This means that these features are an integral part of the model, so if you modify a feature, all parameters are correspondingly modified. For example, suppose that the hole in the handle of the ice scraper has its diameter defined as a function of the handle width. Because the hole is a parametric feature of the model, if the handle width is changed, the hole diameter will change by an appropriate amount. A parametric CAD system such as Designer allows you to easily make changes in your design model and ask "what if" design questions.

When building a complex model, the order of construction is important. When adding features to a 3-D designer model, you should try to add them in the order of most complex to least complex. The software will occasionally be unable to complete an operation when going from simple to more complex and will give you an error message.

Step One: Part Viewing

AutoCAD multiple viewports are a valuable aid when creating and editing a 3-D model. Designer ships with **AutoLisp** routines, which will automatically create between 1 and 4 viewports of your model showing the 3-D model from different points of view. Therefore, you can view the part in primary orthographic views, an isometric view, or a view from the current sketch plane. Before you can use these routines they have to be loaded into AutoCAD using the AutoCAD **load** command. To activate these routines:

    Select: **File>Applications**

From the **Applications** dialog box, select the **File** button. You should see a list of all the AutoLisp files. The adbonus files should be located in the ..\support subdirectory. Select the file **adbonus2.lsp.** This file contains several lisp routines that can be used to automate certain Designer operations.

After you have selected this file, click the mouse on the **Load** button. It should now be loaded and the routines are available for use.

Once you have loaded these routines, you can select multiple viewports by simply typing **1, 2, 3,** or **4** at the Command: prompt followed by ↵. Designer will create the proper number of viewports and allow you to view the model from the primary orthographic and isometric directions.

Step Two: Extruding the Profile to Create a 3-D Solid

Load the file of the ice scraper profile that you created in Chapter 2. Before doing any extrude operations, it is useful to view the 3-D model from different perspectives. After loading the adbonus2.lsp routines discussed above, type in **3** ↵ to automatically create 3 viewports showing the primary orthographic views and an isometric view. Because the profile is only two-dimensional, you will see it as a plane in the isometric view.

Extrusion Options: Base, Cut, Join, Intersect

After creating an initial 3-D base object, you can create additional 2-D profiles to be used in modifying the base object. These profiles act as "templates" for performing Boolean operations such as cut, join, or intersect. When beginning a 3-D model, the first operation that is available is the **Extrude/Base** operation. All other operations are "grayed" out and cannot be used until you first define a base part. The Base operation creates a solid by taking the 2-D profile and adding material in the Z direction to create a 3-D solid. The solid is extruded in the Z direction until terminated by one of four methods:

- The **blind** termination extrudes the feature to a specified depth from the initial profile plane.

- The **mid plane** termination extrudes the profile equally in both directions, terminating at the specified overall depth. When creating the initial base part, the blind and mid plane termination are the only method available.

- When modifying the geometry of the base part, you can terminate the extrusion at the **To Plane** option, which extrudes the profile through a certain depth to a specified planar face or previously defined plane.

- The last termination option, **Through**, is used only when cutting or intersecting the profile with an existing base feature. The through termination will cut entirely through the given part.

Once a base feature is created, the Boolean operations **cut, join, and intersect** can be used to build upon and modify the base part.

- The **cut** operation removes material from the active part, using the 2-D profile as a "cookie cutter."

- The **join** operation adds material to the active part, by extruding the profile through some distance normal to a face on the base part.

- Finally, the **Intersect** operation creates a new feature from the shared volume between the initial base feature and the new profile.

Figures 4-2 and 4-3 illustrate the difference between these different operations on a simple cubic base part. An ellipse profile on the front of the part is used to modify the block during one of these three extrusion operations. Prior to doing any advanced construction operations, you must create the **base**, or fundamental part of your model, in this case a block. The Boolean operations of cut, intersect, or join will not be available until you've first created a base part. This operation is performed by extruding a 2-D profile through some distance. An alternative to extrusion is to create the base part by revolving the profile or sweeping it along a three-dimensional path. Revolve and sweep operations will be covered in later chapters.

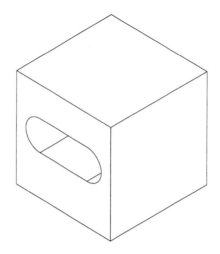

Figure 4-2 *Designer extrude/cut operation*

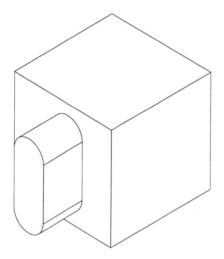

Figure 4-3 *Designer extrude/join operation*

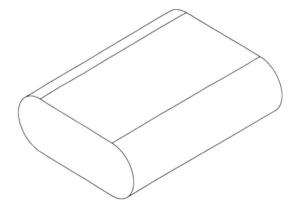

Figure 4-4 *Designer extrude/intersect operation*

Using Extrusion to Create a 3-D Solid Model from the Profile

In the previous chapter you created a fully dimensioned, constrained 2-D profile of an ice scraper. This profile will now be extruded (mass added) in the Z direction to create a solid model of the ice scraper. You will use the **adextrude** command to create a 3-D extrusion from the 2-D profile.

Select: **Designer>Features>Extrude**

In response to this command, you will see the designer extrusion dialog box. The viable options will be highlighted and the other ones automatically grayed out. Since we are starting with the 2-D profile, the only option available is the "base" extrusion. Once a base solid part is created, you can use the other Boolean operations to modify the part. These dialog boxes are "intelligent," and will show graphically what happens to your profile in response to each choice. For the present case, the only choices are to terminate the extrusion at the mid-plane of some thickness, or to extrude the profile **blind** through some distance. The draft angle is the angle of taper as the profile is being extruded. This can be either a positive or negative value.

Complete the dialog box as shown in Figure 4-5 and click **OK** when finished.

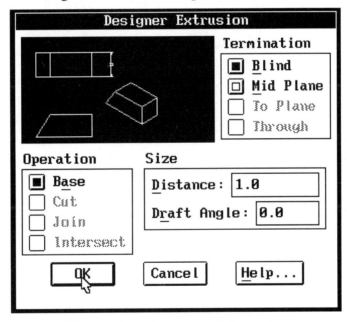

Figure 4-5 *Extrusion dialogue box*

In this case, the thickness or "Z" distance is one unit. Because the draft angle is specified as 0, the shape will have straight sides in the Z direction, orthogonal to the original profile. The object is now a 3-dimensional solid and your screen should look like Figure 4-6.

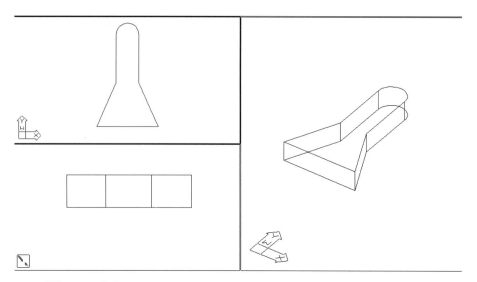

Figure 4-6 *Solid model after extrude "base" operation*

Step Three: Adding 3-D Features to the Model

Chamfers, fillets, and holes are added to the model with intelligent graphical dialog boxes. Because Designer is a **feature based** solid modeler, these are **not** mere geometrical entities such as lines and circles, but are an integral part, or "feature," of the model. Because they form a basis in defining the model, they are created and edited as complete entities. In other words, when editing one of these features, you don't worry about changing all the individual lines, arcs, circles, etc., you simply select the feature and change the appropriate entries in the context sensitive dialogue box. The model can be edited with only a few clicks of the mouse! To illustrate how easy you can create these features using Designer, you will add a hole to the handle of the ice scraper model.

Adding a Hole

The **adhole** command is used to add a hole to any Designer model. Designer will automatically create a drilled, counterbore, or countersunk hole on any face of the 3-D solid model. The defining parameters for this hole are input with a context sensitive dialogue box.

   Select: **Designer>Features>Hole**

   A designer hole dialog box will appear, with the viable options highlighted. Certain operations may be grayed out. You have a choice of three hole types: drilled, counterbore, or countersunk. The graphic in the dialog box changes as you select different options. You also have a choice of drilling the hole all the way through the model, or terminating it some given distance (blind). The diameter can be specified for the hole and counterbore dimensions. Three options are available for placing the hole: concentric, displaced from two edges, or on a given workpoint in the model. The **Concentric** option will place the hole at a given distance concentric to some circular feature. The 2 edges option will place the hole on a planar surface with the centerpoint located a given distance from two edges. The last choice, On Point, will place the centerpoint on top of a user-defined work point. User-defined work points will be covered in later chapters.

Complete the dialog box as shown in Figure 4-7 and click OK when finished.

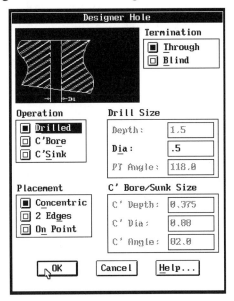

Figure 4-7 *Designer Hole dialogue box*

After completing this dialogue box you will be prompted with:

Select work plane or planar face: *Select a line on the face where you will locate the hole. The face should be highlighted (a dotted line). If you select an edge common to more than one face, you may have to toggle through the faces by selecting the **Next** option.*

Select concentric edge: *Select the curved surface at the top of the scraper.*

After completing these steps, your scraper should have a hole drilled through the handle.

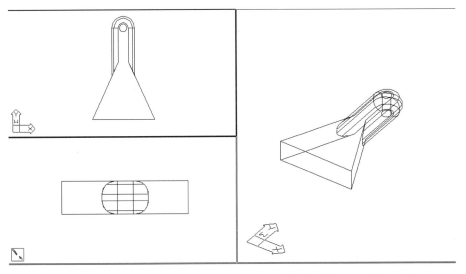

Figure 4-8 *Ice scraper with "hole" drilled through handle*

Filleting the Handle

The **adfillet** command will apply a fillet to any edge in the 3-D model. Unlike the conventional AutoCAD fillet command, you do not have to select two lines to locate the fillet. You simply select the edge you wish to fillet and input a fillet radius. Generally it works best to use an isometric view of your model when selecting edges or features. Using the pull-down menus:

Select: **Designer>Features>Fillet**

Select edge: *Select an edge.* ↵

Select edge: *You may select another edge or press return.*

Fillet radius: *Enter a value of .4 for the fillet radius.* ↵

If the geometry of the 3-D edge to too complex, the following error message will appear:

```
geometry or topology at end of bend too complex

Could not execute fillet.
```

You may be able to fillet complex geometry by changing the order in which you apply the features. The **adfillet** command works best on simple geometry. Try removing a previous complex feature and applying the fillet first.

If the fillet radius is too large for some small edges, you may get the following error message:

```
spring curves do not intersect

Could not execute fillet.
```

You may be able to apply a fillet by specifying a smaller value for the radius. When finished, your ice scraper should have a filleted edge on the handle.

Applying a Chamfer to the Blade

Like the features we've previously added to our model, Designer uses a graphical dialogue box to create a chamfer on any 3-D edges. To add the chamfer which brings the blade to a sharp edge, type the command:

Command: adchamfer ↵ *or use the pull-down menus:*

Select: **Designer>Features>Chamfer**

The designer chamfer dialogue box will appear giving you the options shown below. Again, the graphic in this box changes in response to the type of operation selected. The chamfer can be specified by inputting one value for both equal distances, two distances independently, or a distance and angle. Complete the box so it looks like the one shown in Figure 4-9 and click **OK** when finished.

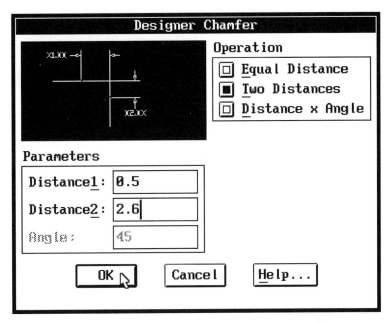

Figure 4-9 *Designer Chamfer dialogue box*

The cursor is now active to select an edge to cut.

Select edge: *Pick the bottom face. (You will probably find that the best view for selecting these edges is the isometric.)*

Flip/(Accept): ↵ *To flip, type* **F↵,** *or return to accept. This command toggles the face that you will chamfer. The correct face is highlighted by a "dashed" line. The correct face should be the bottom surface of the chamfer. When this one is highlighted, type* **A↵** *to accept.*

If you make the chamfer too large for the model a modeling error will appear:

Modeling error: blend radius too big for adjacent face, or edge curvature. Could not construct feature.

This operation only chamfers one face of the blade and will have to be repeated to cut the other face to a sharp edge. Repeat this operation for the other face of the blade so your scraper looks like the one shown in Figure 4-10. As a shortcut, use the **Enter** key or the **right mouse button** to repeat an AutoCAD command.

Select edge: *Select the bottom face.*

If the wrong face highlights, use the *flip* command to get the correct face (this should be the bottom of the scraper).

Flip/<Accept>: *flip↵*

Press **A** ↵ to accept and apply the chamfer.

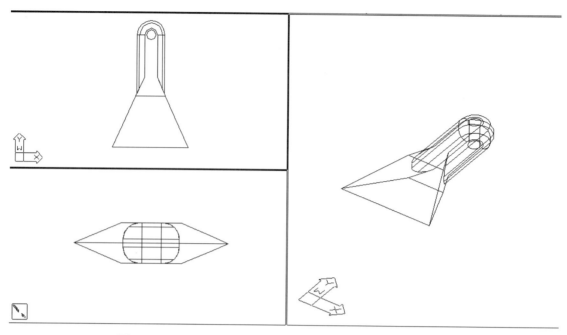

Figure 4-10 *Chamfer applied to both faces of blade*

Deleting a Feature

Use the **addelfeat** command to remove features applied to the object. Any Designer features such as holes, chamfers, or fillets can be removed from the model with this command. To apply this command type:

Select: **Designer>Features>Delete**

Select feature to delete: *Use the mouse to select the feature to delete.*

*Note: If you apply a given feature more than once to your model, this command will remove **all** features that were applied at that step.*

Editing Features

The **adeditfeat** command can be used to edit Designer features. You can use this command to change a dimension on a feature or to change the size and type of hole. The **adeditfeat** command is context sensitive, and you will be prompted in the appropriate context of the feature you are trying to edit. If you select a dimension in response to this command, then the dimension can be changed. If you select a hole in response to **adeditfeat**, then the Designer hole dialogue box will appear and you can change parameters in the box.

Select: **Designer>Edit Feature**

Select feature: *Use the mouse to select a feature.*

Upon activating a feature, Designer will highlight all the parametric dimensions used to define that feature. To change a dimension, use the mouse to select one of the highlighted dimensions.

Select dimension to change: *Select a dimension with the mouse.*

New value for dimension <#>: *Type in a new value for the dimension.*

You can continue modifying dimensions in the selected feature. Press ↵ when finished to complete this operation. Since the model now has *pending edits*, you need to execute the **adupdate** command to apply the changes to the complete model. Since you are editing a complete solid model rather than individual geometric entities, any changes to one of these features affects all other geometry in the model.

Upon executing the **adupdate** command Designer evaluates all geometrical constraints and updates the model. Any associated drawing views are also updated automatically.

If You're New to AutoCAD: Plotting a Drawing

The AutoCAD **plot** command is used to plot the drawings you've created so far. This command can be accessed from the pull-down menus through the **File>Plot...** menu, or you can type **plot** at the **Command**: prompt. The Plot dialogue box is then used to set up plotting parameters and preview your plot on the screen before sending it to the plotter.

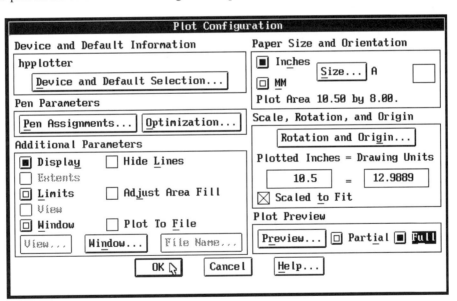

Normally you will plot the **display**, which creates a plot of what's on your screen. Occasionally, you may check the **Window** box, which will plot only a window that you place around a portion of your drawing. **Scaled to Fit** will automatically scale the plot so that it fits on the sheet of paper that is in your plotter. Sometimes you may want to plot a drawing so that the actual plotted drawing size is in scale with the units you used to create the drawing. For these cases, be sure to "uncheck" the **Scaled to Fit** box and type an appropriate scaling factor between the plotted inches and drawing units (for example, 1 to 1). It is a good idea to do a plot preview before actually sending your drawing to the plotter. A **Full** plot preview will show you on the computer screen exactly how your drawing will fit inside the margins of the paper. You can then make adjustments before sending it to the plotter.

End of Chapter Summary

You've taken the two-dimensional profile of the ice scraper and extruded it to create a three-dimensional solid model. You've added a hole, fillet, and chamfer to the blade using the Designer's interactive dialog boxes. Because the model is parametric, you can modify any dimension or feature in your model, and all associated geometry is correspondingly modified. In the next chapter you will use this solid model as a basis for creating conventional engineering drawings (2-dimensional).

Exercises

Use Designer's 3-D extrusion options to construct the following solid models. Use the dimensions shown.

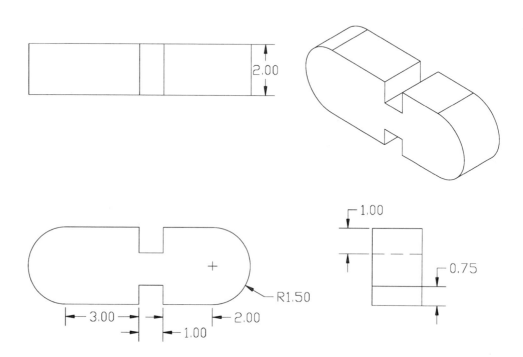

Ex 4-1

Exercises 67

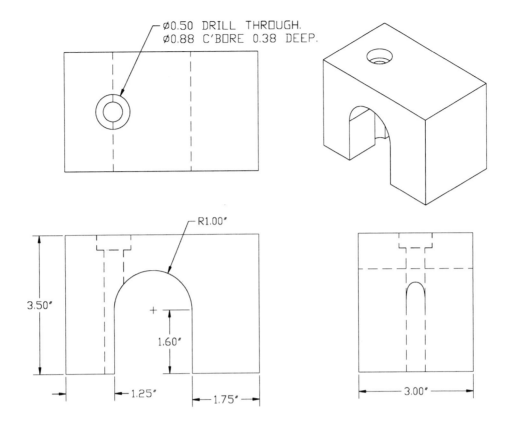

Ex 4-2

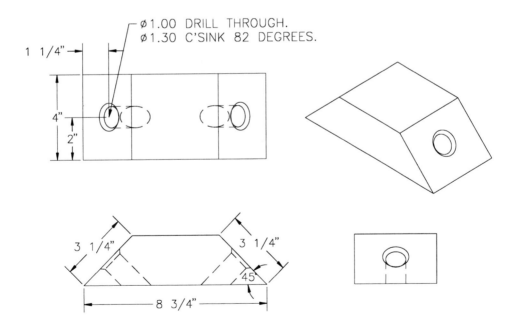

Ex 4-3

68 Creating a 3-D Solid Model from a 2-D Profile

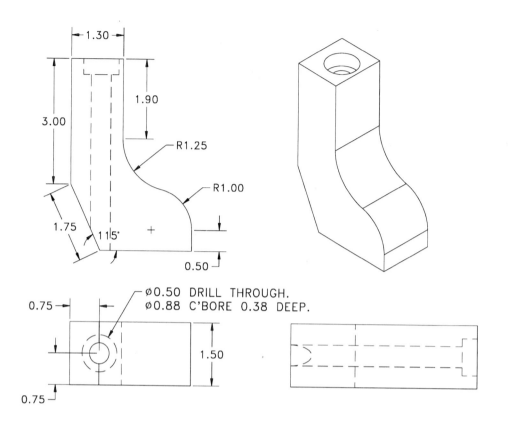

Ex 4-4

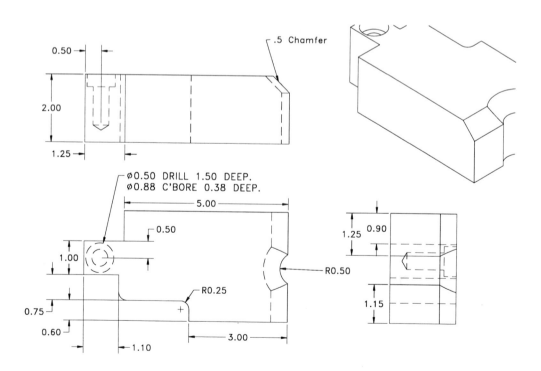

Ex 4-5

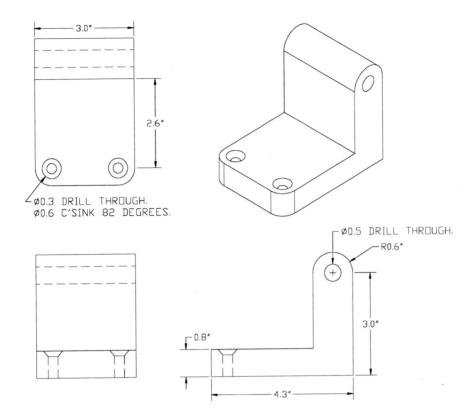

Ex 4-6

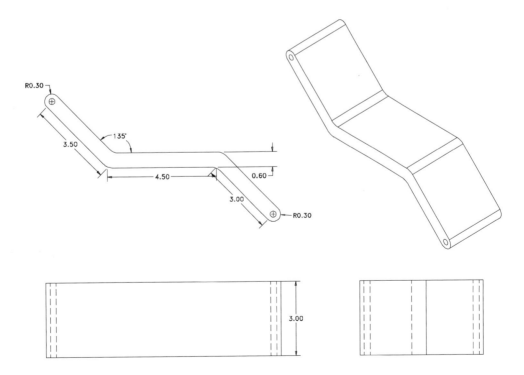

Ex 4-7

70 Creating a 3-D Solid Model from a 2-D Profile

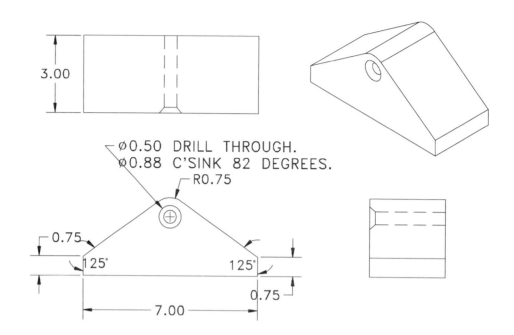

Ex 4-8

Chapter 5

Creating 2-D Views from a 3-D Model

When you have completed this lesson you will:

1. **Understand how to create a "paper space" drawing from a Designer 3-D model.**
2. **Be able to create conventional orthographic drawings from the 3-D model.**
3. **Be able to create isometric, auxiliary, cross-sectional, and detail drawings from the 3-D model.**
4. **Be able to insert information such as dimensions, hole notes, and annotations into the 2-D drawings.**
5. **Be able to add, delete, and modify the 2-D drawings.**

Introduction

The ice scraper you've created in previous chapters is not a *drawing*, but is rather a completely defined, unambiguous, and geometrically consistent *solid model* representing the ice scraper. At some point in the design process, engineers will most likely need to document the geometric model they've created using conventional two-dimensional "paper" drawings. Designer supports several automatic drafting features, which allow you to quickly take off conventional two-dimensional views from the 3-D model. The software supports automatic generation of orthographic views, isometric views, detail drawings, auxiliary views, and sectional views.

Because the solid model represents a complete, fully defined geometric model of your design, it contains all relevant data such as dimensions, sizes, locations, and mass properties. This information can easily and automatically be inserted into the 2-D drawings for quick documentation of your design. In this lesson you will create conventional 2-D "working drawings" from the 3-D model of the ice scraper created in the previous lessons. You will use Designer's automatic drafting features to annotate and edit these drawings.

Designer supports **bi-directional associativity** between the two-dimensional drawing views and the three-dimensional solid model. This means that all 2-D views are directly linked to the 3-D model. You can change a dimension on one of the 2-D views and the corresponding dimension in the model will also be modified. If the 3-D model is modified, all related views on the 2-D drawing are automatically updated to reflect these changes. These features allow for very rapid documentation of your design solution.

When creating a drawing, Designer operates in two different states: **Part Mode** and **Drawing Mode**. Drawing mode represents a sheet of paper, and you see the 2-D views exactly as they'll look when plotted. Various Designer commands automate the creation of views from the 3-D model. Part mode is used for creating and editing the 3-D model. To switch modes, you can use the **Designer>Mode** pull-down menu, or type **admode↵** at the **Command**: prompt.

Creating and Editing Views

Before beginning this tutorial, load in the ice scraper model you created in the previous chapters. Use the AutoCAD **open** command to load this file.

Creating the base view

Designer will automatically create all types of engineering drawings from the 3-D model, including all the primary orthographic views, isometric views, detail views, and sections. When beginning a drawing, the first view you must create is the **base view**. The base view is an orthographic reference view of the model, which is the basis for all other views. You can define the base view of the model from any direction or viewpoint in 3-D space. Generally, you will select a planar face of your model to represent the base view.

To create the base views from the solid model, use the **adview** command. You can type **adview** at the **command**: prompt or you can use the pull-down menus.

Select: **Designer>Drawing>Create View**

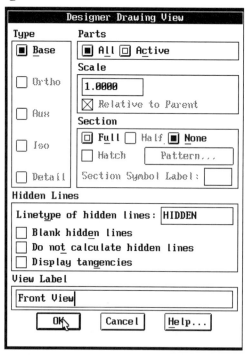

Figure 5-1 *Designer Drawing View dialogue box*

In response to entering the **adview** command, you will see the Designer Drawing View dialogue box as shown in Figure 5-1. The only option available initially is the Base view type. All other options are grayed out. Once you've created the base view, you can build ortho, iso, auxiliary, or sectional views off of this view and these options will be available in the dialogue box. Notice some of the options available. You can scale the drawing by some factor, type in a view title, select a hatch pattern from the AutoCAD pattern library, and include/exclude hidden lines. When creating ortho views, the views are automatically aligned according to the rules of orthographic projection. In order to get your views to fit properly on an "A" size sheet, you may have to enter a view scale of **.5** (half sized). If you are using a larger plotter, then you can leave the view scale at a factor of 1.000 (default). If you want the view to be labeled, enter **Front View** in the label box.

You will be prompted with:

Xy/Yz/Zx/Ucs: <Select work plane or planer face>: *Click on any edge that lies on the face you wish to build this view from, or select some point on the face. For this exercise, pick point P1 in Figure 5-2.*

Designer will highlight one planar face of your model. If you select an edge, the edge will be common to two different surfaces. Therefore, the wrong surface or face may be highlighted. If the wrong face is highlighted, you can toggle through the faces by selecting the *Next* option until you have the proper face selected.

Rotate/(Accept): ↵ (>: *You will see an icon representing the X and Y axes of the drawing you are creating. You can rotate the X and Y axes for the drawing view by typing **R**. The Y axis always points toward the "top" of the paper. Type in an **R** until the icon is aligned properly, then type an **A** to accept.)*

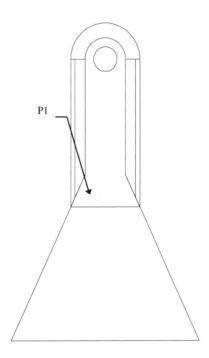

Figure 5-2 *Pick point P1 for creating base view*

After executing the last command you will be automatically switched to drawing mode, which initially represents a blank sheet of paper. If this is the first view in the drawing, the screen will initially be blank. You will then be prompted with:

view center: *Use the mouse to locate where in the drawing you want to place the center of this view.* ↵

If You're New to AutoCAD: Loading a Drawing Prototype File

When you start a new drawing in AutoCAD, a **prototype drawing file** is normally loaded automatically before you start the drawing. Any existing drawing can be used as a prototype. The prototype drawing contains basic settings and can contain a template to be used as a border and title block for your drawing. The default prototype file is **acad.dwg**, which is included with AutoCAD. Designer has available another prototype file, **adesign.dwg,** which has many features and settings pre-defined to assist you in creating a Designer drawing. The **adesign.dwg** file contains a pre-defined border and title block that will assist you in creating a professional looking drawing. You can load this file as your prototype through the **Create New Drawing** dialogue box which appears every time you start a new drawing from scratch.

To select the **adesign.dwg** file as your prototype file, click the mouse in the **Prototype** box. You will see a list of prototype drawing files. Select the **adesign.dwg** file and click **OK** with the mouse. If you would like this file to become your default prototype drawing, which is automatically loaded every time you start a new drawing, be sure to check the **Retain as Default** box.

Your screen should look like Figure 5-3. The border and title block are part of the **adesign.dwg** prototype file which ships with Designer. If you did not load this file as your prototype file when creating a new model, then your screen will initially be blank.

The view you just created is called the parent view and forms the basis for all other two-dimensional views.

Creating and Editing Views **75**

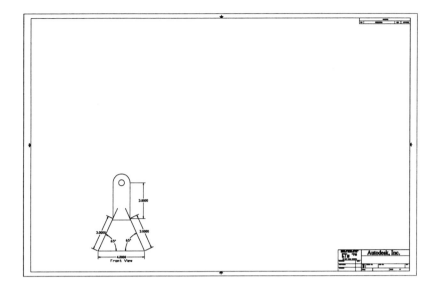

Figure 5-3 *Creating a "parent view" in paper space*

Adding Other Views

Right side view

Once you've established a base view, you can repeat the **adview** command to create other 2-D views from the base view. You will see the same dialogue box, but the other options will not be grayed out.

> Select: **Designer>Drawings>Create View** from the pull-down menus. *Note: A short cut when creating multiple views is to press the right mouse button. This repeats the previous AutoCAD command, in this case the **adview** command.*

Complete the dialogue box so that it looks like the one shown in Figure 5-4. Click **OK** when finished. Be sure to fill in the **View Label** box.

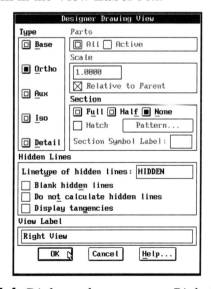

Figure 5-4 *Dialogue box to create Right Side View*

76 Creating 2-D Views from a 3-D Model

You will receive the following prompts:

Select parent view: *Choose the base view.*

Location of orthographic view: *Use the mouse to place the view to the right of the base view.*

Location of orthographic view: ↵

Notice that the proper ortho view is automatically created from the parent view based upon how you orient the mouse. When creating an orthographic view, Designer constrains the view location to be orthogonal with the base or parent view. If the location was selected above the parent view, then the top bottom view would be automatically created. Hidden and centerlines are automatically placed in the drawing. This is shown in Figure 5-5.

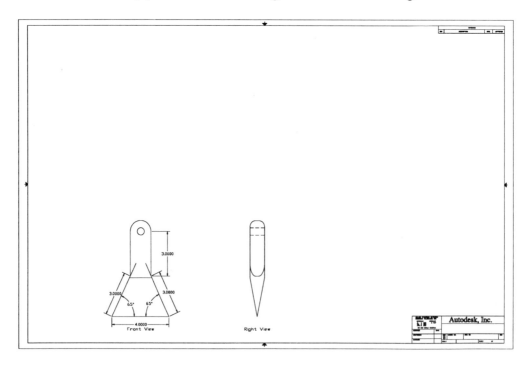

Figure 5-5 *Creating Right View*

Top view

The process is repeated to create the top view. The only changes are in the view label entered in the Designer View dialogue box and the location of the orthographic view. Because you place the view location above the parent front, Designer will automatically create a top view. This is shown in Figure 5-6.

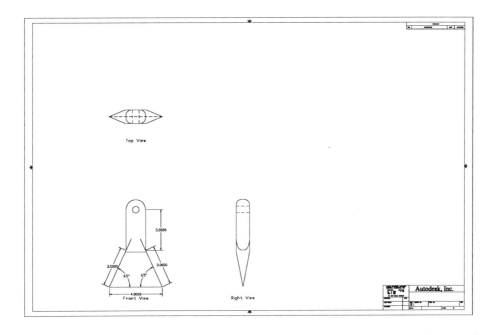

Figure 5-6 *Creating Top View*

Creating an isometric view

An isometric view is created in much the same way as the ortho views. The **adview** command is executed to bring up the same dialogue box (for a shortcut, press the right mouse button or Enter key to repeat the previous AutoCAD command). Notice that when an **iso** view is selected, the default for hidden lines is to blank hidden lines. This box can be "unchecked" if you want hidden lines to be included in the isometric view. If you want the iso view to be the same size as the other views on your drawing, be sure that the entry in the Scale field is **1.000**. After entering information into the appropriate fields, click the OK button.

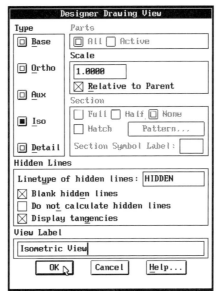

Figure 5-7 *Drawing View Dialogue box to create an isometric view*

You will then be prompted with:

Select parent view: *Choose the front view as the base view. The orientation of the isometric view depends upon which ortho view you use for the parent view.*

Location of isometric view: *Use the mouse to place the view in an empty location.*

Location of isometric view: ↵

The isometric view should be automatically generated in the location you select. Remember, if the view is not the way you want it, the easiest way to make a correction is to use the AutoCAD **Undo** and repeat the last operation. Your completed two-dimensional drawings should look like Figure 5-8. The parametric dimensions that you used to define the base profile are automatically added to the appropriate views. Some of the features may not be dimensioned, so you can use special Designer commands to add those dimensions and annotations. These commands will be covered later in this chapter.

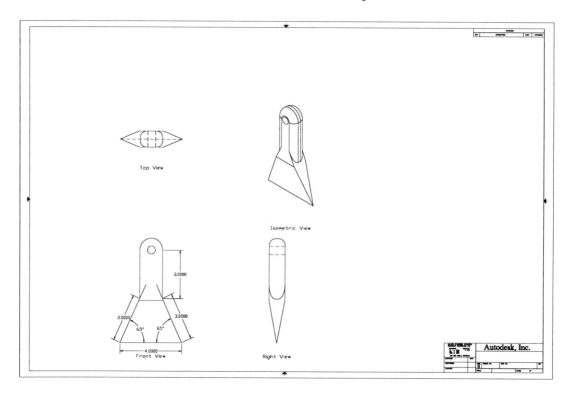

Figure 5-8 *Complete multi-view drawing of ice scraper*

Editing Views

If you need to modify or edit any views, it is important that you use the Designer **Edit View** commands. *Do not* use conventional AutoCAD editing commands such as **erase, move, rotate, copy,** etc. These commands may appear to work on a Designer drawing, but will most likely produce erratic and unpredictable results, particularly if you modify the model. Designer has special commands to be used to move, delete, annotate, and add dimensions to a view.

Creating and Editing Views

Moving a view

The **admoveview** command can be used to move a view in the drawing. To use this command type:

Select: **Designer>Drawing>Edit View>Move View**

Select view to move: *Click the left mouse button anywhere on the appropriate view.*

View location: *Use the mouse to select a new location. You can continue to move the view until the ↵ key is pressed.*

View location: ↵ *(This establishes the new location.)*

Deleting a view

The **addelview** command is used to delete a view. *Do not* use an AutoCAD **erase** command to delete a view. The **erase** command does not completely remove all the Designer data represented by the view and will cause unpredictable results if you make changes in your drawing. You can type **addelview** at the **command**: prompt, or use the pull-down menus to delete a view.

Select: **Designer>Drawing>Edit View>Delete**

Select view to delete: *Click the left mouse button anywhere in the view to remove.*

If the view you are trying to delete is the parent for other views, Designer will prompt you if you want to delete the children views also.

Changing the attributes of a view

The **aeditview** command allows you to change the attributes of a view such as the scale, linetypes, attributes of hidden lines, and the view label. Upon executing this command you will see a dialogue box like the one shown in Figure 5-9.

Select: **Designer>Drawing>Edit View>Attributes**

Select view: *Use the mouse to select the view to edit.*

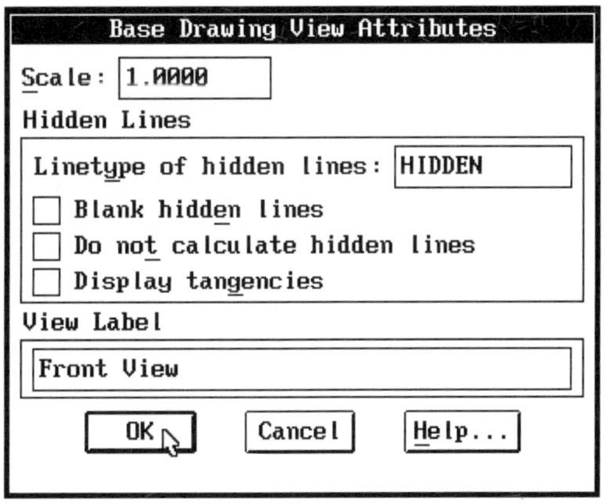

Figure 5-9 *Edit View Attributes dialogue box*

Adding Dimensions to the Drawing

When creating orthographic views from the model, Designer will automatically place dimensions on the views which correspond to the parametric dimensions used to create the model. Occasionally, you may find it necessary to show more dimensions in your drawing. The **adrefdim** command can be used to add reference dimensions to any feature in one of the orthographic views. Reference dimensions show the size or location of a feature, much like conventional AutoCAD dimensions. They are not **parametric dimensions**, meaning that you cannot change the geometry of the model by modifying the reference dimensions. To execute this command, type **adrefdim** from the **Command**: prompt or use the pull-down menus:

Select: **Designer>Drawing>Dimension>Ref Dim**

Select first item: *Select item that you wish to dimension in one of the ortho views.*

Select second item or place dimension: *Select the location for the dimension.*

Specify dimension placement: *Specify where to place the dimension.*

Undo/Ref/Basic/Placement point: *Specify the type of dimension.*

Changing Dimensions

Because Designer drawings support **bi-directional associativity**, you can edit any of the parametric dimensions in the drawing view, and the model's geometry will be automatically updated to reflect the new values of the dimension. Use the **admoddim** command to change dimensions. The only dimensions that can be edited are the parametric dimensions, which define the model and its features. These are the dimensions that were used to define the initial profile. Because the geometric model is parametric, if one dimension is changed, all other dimensions and features are correspondingly updated. This means the lines continue to remain orthogonal, parallel, etc. Before these changes are reflected in the drawings and the on-screen representation of the 3-D model, you must execute the **adupdate** command. This command updates all related geometry in response to any changes you make.

Select: **Designer>Change Dimension**

Select dimension to change: *Use the left mouse button to select a dimension.*

New value for dimension <3>: **4.↵**

Command: **adupdate.↵** *(This command updates all features to correspond to the new value of the dimension.)*

Dimensions can also be edited directly from the model by switching back to **Part** mode. Use the **admode** command to switch from drawing back to **Part** mode.

Command: **admode.↵**

Part/(Drawing): **p.↵**

You are now in **Part** mode. Use the **adeditfeat** to change the dimensions of that feature. When you select a feature to edit, all relevant dimensions are highlighted.

Select: **Designer>Edit Feature**

Select feature: *Use the left mouse button to any geometry of the feature you want to change. When this feature is activated, all relevant dimensions will be highlighted.*

Select dimension to change: *Pick one of the highlighted dimensions with the left mouse button. You will see the current value of that dimension in the < > brackets.*

New value for dimension <current value>: *Enter a new value for this dimension.*

Select dimension to change: ↵

Command: **adupdate**↵ *(This command will update all geometry in the model **and** the drawings to reflect the changes you've made.)*

The model will *not* automatically update when you edit or change dimensions and features. The **adupdate** command must be executed to see the changes carried through to all of the geometry. Because Designer uses bi-directional associativity *both* the model and the drawing are updated simultaneously to reflect these changes. The complete fully dimensioned drawing is shown in Figure 5-10.

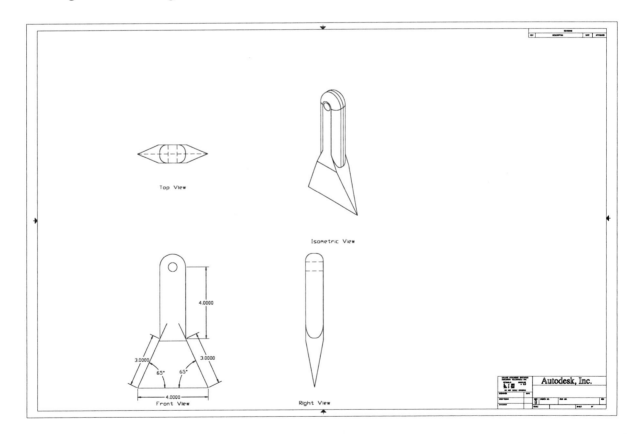

Figure 5-10 *Ice scraper drawing with dimensions edited*

Moving Dimensions

The parametric dimensions that you used to define the model are automatically placed on the appropriate view when creating a drawing from your model. Designer locates these dimensions in the drawing exactly where you located them when defining the profile. When creating multiple views of the part, these dimensions may need to be moved or switched to another view to prevent a cluttered drawing. You may find that some of the dimensions show up on top of each other, or that by moving them to another view, the drawing will appear less cluttered. The Designer **admovedim** command can be used to move or relocate dimensions to another view. The AutoCAD **move** command cannot be used to move dimensions. To illustrate, we will move one of the 4″ vertical dimensions for the ice scraper handle to a different view. To execute this command, type **admovedim** at the **command**: prompt or use the pull-down menus:

Select: **Designer>Drawing>Dimension>Move**

Reattach/<Select dimension>: *Select any point on the vertical 4″ dimension.*

Select view to place dimension: *Select the right side view. (Note: If you only want to relocate the dimension text, then select the same view.)*

Location for dimension: *Select a new location for the dimension.*

The dimension should now be placed in the right side view.

Hole Notes

The **adholenote** command is used to annotate the drawing and specify standard hole notes. Hole notes can be placed in any view. When you select a hole for annotation, Designer will list all relevant information about that hole, since holes are treated as features rather than unrelated geometric entities.

Select: **Designer>Drawing>Annotation>Hole Note**

Select arc or circle of hole feature: *Pick the circle at the top.*

Location for hole note: *Place the note in an empty location, i.e., to the right.*

Location for hole note: ↵

Notice how Designer automatically generates the hole note based upon the type of hole you selected when creating the "hole" feature. If you modify this hole, the hole note will be automatically updated to reflect the new hole parameters.

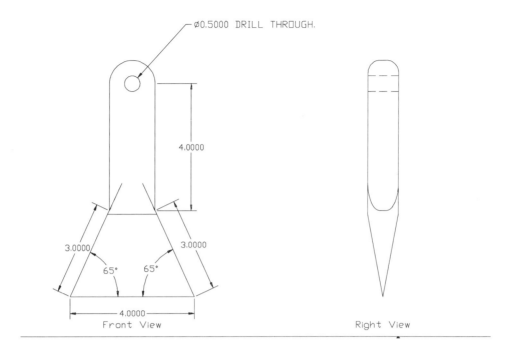

Figure 5-11 *Adding a Designer "hole note"*

Using Designer's Automatic Cross-sectioning Features

Designer will create automatic cross sections using either a work plane or a point on the part to define the cutting plane. The points are restricted to either the centerpoints of circles and arcs, or the endpoints of edges. Since work planes will not be covered until the next chapter, we will use the centerpoint of the circle in the handle of the ice scraper to define a cutting plane.

To illustrate automatic cross sectioning, you will delete the right side view of the ice scraper and re-create this view as a full section.

To delete the right side, use the **addelview** command. You can type **addelview** at the **Command**: prompt, or use the pull-down menus to delete a view.

Select: **Designer>Drawing>Edit View>Delete**

Select view to delete: *Click the left mouse button anywhere in the right side view to remove.*

Use the **adview** command to create the cross-sectional view. This command will be used as if creating an orthographic view, but the **full section** box will be selected in the **Create View** dialogue box.

Select **Designer>Drawing>Create View**

84 Creating 2-D Views from a 3-D Model

Complete the **Create View** dialogue box so the full **Section** and **Hatch** pattern boxes are checked. The dialogue box should look like Figure 5-12. Choose an ANSI31 pattern for the cross section. Use **A** for the section label.

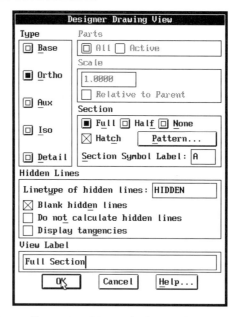

Figure 5-12 *Designer Drawing View dialogue box to create a cross section*

Choose **OK** to close the Designer Drawing View dialogue box. Designer returns you to drawing mode.

Select parent view: *Pick any point on the front view of the ice scraper.*

Location for orthographic view: *Pick a point to the right of the front view.*

Location for orthographic view: *Press ↵.*

Section through Point/<Work Plane>: **P↵** *(The default is to use a work plane for the cutting plane. For this example, you will pick the centerpoint of the circle in the handle, so type P↵).*

Select point in parent view for the section: *Pick the hole in the front view to define a cutting plane through the centerpoint of the circle.*

Designer should create a right side view of the ice scraper with an ANSI31 hatch pattern representing the cross section. Since you specified the **Section through Point** option to locate the cutting plane, the plane is automatically created through the hole, using the *A* symbol that we defined in the dialogue box. If you add work planes to the drawing, they can also be used to locate the cutting planes. Your drawing should look like Figure 5-13.

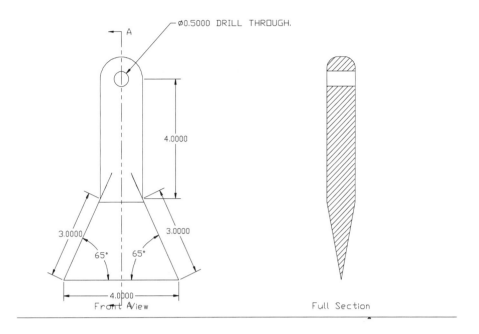

Figure 5-13 *Cross sectional orthographic view*

Creating Auxiliary Views

Auxiliary views are needed when the part you are creating has planes or surfaces that are not parallel or normal to one of the principle orthographic views. Therefore, the true size of these surfaces will be distorted in one of their primary orthographic views. You can show the true size of a given face by picking an edge bounding that face in the parent view. Designer will create an auxiliary view perpendicular to that edge. The attributes and scale of the auxiliary view are determined by the scale and attributes of the parent view.

To illustrate the creation of an auxiliary view, we will use the tapered blade of the ice scraper as the parent surface for an auxiliary view. The auxiliary view will then show that edge in its true size. Before creating an auxiliary view, you need to make room for that view by deleting the isometric view previously created.

Use the **addelview** command to delete the isometric view.

Use the **adview** command to open the Designer **Drawing View** dialogue box (or use the pull-down menus):

Select: **Designer>Drawings>Create View** from the pull-down menus.

For the view type, select **Aux**. Designer will display the following prompt:

Select a straight edge in the parent view. *Select point P1, in the edge of the ice scraper blade, as shown in Figure 5-14.*

Select second point or <RETURN> to use the selected edge: *Press ↵ to complete the selection.*

Location for auxiliary view: *Pick point P2, which will project the auxiliary view to the right of the parent view. ↵ completes the selection.*

Your auxiliary view should look like Figure 5-14.

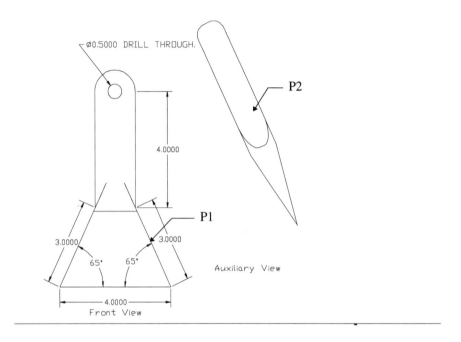

Figure 5-14 *Auxiliary view of ice scraper blade*

Creating Detail Views

If you need to see an enlarged detail of the part, Designer will create detail views. These views can be scaled differently than the parent view. They can be used to show small details and dimensions of certain features of the part. The orientation of a detail view is the same as that of the parent view.

To create a detail view, use the same **adview** command you used to create all the other views. Be sure the **Detail** box is checked in the Designer Drawing View dialogue box. You can specify a scale factor for the view relative to the parent view, or you can specify an absolute scale factor by "unchecking" the Relative to Parent box. Designer will prompt you to drag a box around the area you want to include in the detail view.

End of Chapter Summary

You have just completed a 3-D parametric solid model of an ice scraper, including a set of engineering drawings. You built this model in much the same way as you would solve an engineering design problem. You started with a sketch of the basic shape of the part. Next, the geometry was completely defined and dimensions were added to the sketch. The third step was to create a three-dimensional representation of this part. The fourth step was refinement: you added finishing touches and features such as holes and fillets. Finally, you created a complete set of engineering working drawings for the documentation of this design. Once you'd established the relationship between the drawings and the model, Designer's bi-directional associativity allowed you to edit the drawing and see corresponding changes made in the actual solid model.

Exercises

For the following problems, create a model of the following objects using Designer. Use the Designer **Create Drawing** feature to construct a layout similar to the ones shown below.

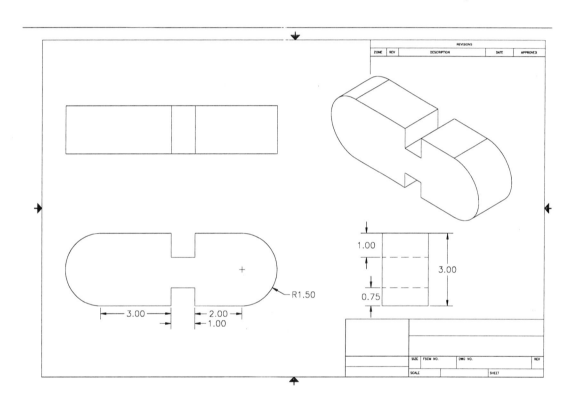

Ex 5-1

88 Creating 2-D Views from a 3-D Model

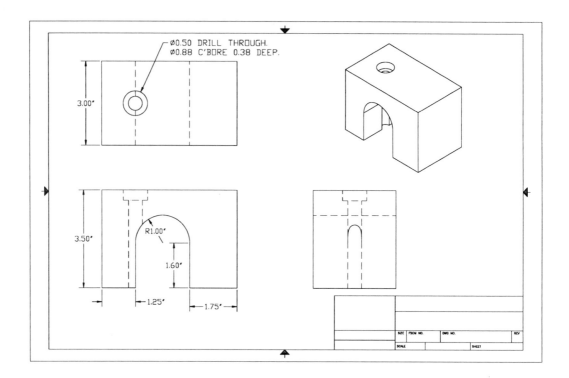

Ex 5-2

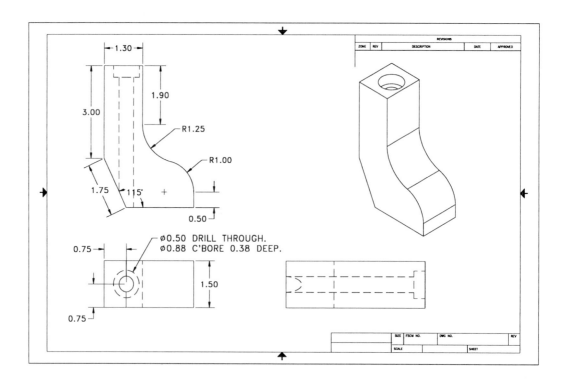

Ex 5-3

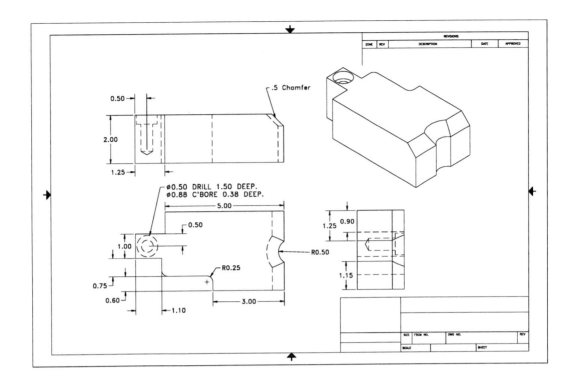

Ex 5-4

Chapter 6

Advanced 3-D Construction: A Chain Rivet Extractor

When you have completed this lesson you will:

1. **Understand how to use 3-D construction aids such as work planes, sketch planes, and work axes**
2. **Use Boolean operators for complex 3-D construction**
3. **Revolve a profile for advanced 3-D construction**

Introduction

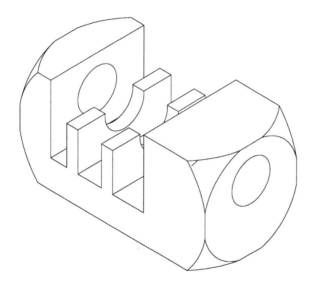

Figure 6-1 *Chain Rivet Extractor*

This lesson illustrates how to use Designer for complex 3-D modeling. You will create a 3-D model of the chain rivet extractor shown in the above illustration. You will learn how to use and manipulate **work planes, work axes,** and **sketch planes.** A profile will be "revolved" about an axis to create the rounded corners in Figure 6-1. You will also practice using the other basic commands you have learned in previous lessons. Using Boolean extrusion operations, you will combine profiles to create complex 3-D shapes.

Like the ice scraper model in previous chapters, this model begins with a basic 2-dimensional profile. Parametric dimensions will be added to the profile, and then extruded to form the basic shape of the chain rivet extractor. Work planes will be defined to assist you in creating complex 3-D geometry. After completing this tutorial, you should see how easy it is to build complex 3-D parts using Designer.

Step One: Create a 2-D Sketch

Begin by creating a sketch of the profile for the part you are going to create. (Remember: Use conventional AutoCAD drawing and editing commands to create the sketch) This is just a sketch, so don't be concerned about exact locations and dimensions. The lines do not have to connect and be exactly orthogonal. However, if you draw the sketch "approximately" the size and shape of the final profile, the process of adding parametric dimensions seems to work better.

Command: **pline**↵

Draw a sketch of the profile of the part similar to the one shown below.

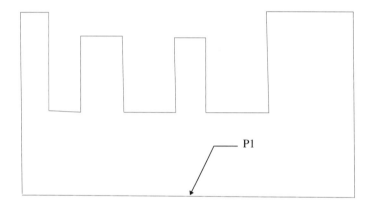

Figure 6-2 *"Rough" sketch of the rivet extractor*

Your sketch should look something like the one in the above diagram. Be careful to make the lines collinear which should be collinear. When designer "solves" this sketch it will automatically apply collinear constraints to the lines which are "close" to being collinear. If you do not make all of the horizontal lines "close" enough to collinear, collinear constraints can be added later. However, it is easier to use care in creating the sketch, thereby minimizing changes you must do later in the modeling process.

Step Two: Create a Profile from the Sketch

Use the **adprofile** command you learned in previous lessons to create a Designer profile.

Select: **Designer>Sketch>Profile** *from pull-down menus*

Select objects: *Select all of the 2-D geometry (if you used a polyline to draw the sketch, you need only select a single point anywhere on the polyline).*

Click the right mouse button

Designer will generate the message:

Introduction 93

`Solved under constrained sketch requiring 10 dimensions / constraints.`

If Designer specifies more than 10 dimensions/constraints, then you probably did not draw all of the horizontal lines collinear, so a collinear constraint was not applied to those lines. To check the constraints applied by Designer, execute the **adshowcon** command. You can either type this command at the **command**: prompt, or use the pull-down menus:

Select **Designer>Sketch>Constraints>Show** *from the pull-down menus.*

All/Select/Next/<exit>: *Type* **A** *to show all the constraints.* ↵

Your profile should look like the one shown in Figure 6-3. Notice the **C#** constraints applied to the upper horizontal lines. If you initially drew these lines "close" to collinear, Designer should have constrained them as being collinear. If Designer did not apply collinear constraints, use the **adaddcon** (see Chapter 3) command to add collinear constraints to these lines.

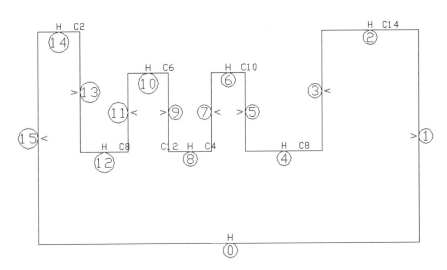

Figure 6-3 *Constrained profile of chain rivet extractor*

After verifying that the geometric constraints were properly added by Designer, you are ready to add parametric dimensions to the sketch.

Select: **Designer>Sketch>Add Dimension** *from the pull-down menus.*

Select first item: *Select P1 (see Figure 6.2)*

Select second item or place dimension: *Place the dimension on the bottom of the sketch.*

Designer will prompt you for the dimension value. The current value will be displayed after the prompt in the format <XX.XX>

Undo/Hor/Ver/Align/Par/Dimension value: **6.0**↵

`Solved under constrained sketch requiring 9 dimensions/constraints.`

Add the rest of the dimensions on the 2-D sketch according to Figure 6.4. Remember, you can select an individual entity and then "place the dimension" to specify a length for that line, or you can specify the distance between two entities, by the "select second item" option. (Refer to Chapter 2 for help.)

Hint: Do the inside dimensions first; the other ones will then be easier. If you make a mistake, use the AutoCAD **Undo** command to "back up." You can also erase a dimension and then continue to add them with the **adpardim** command. If you inadvertently select a dimension extension line, Designer will tell you that it "can't attach dimension." Try selecting the entity from another direction, or try changing the order in which you add dimensions.

If You're New to AutoCAD: The Undo Command

The AutoCAD **Undo** command is a powerful editing feature to use when creating a Designer model. When creating and editing an AutoCAD drawing, the commands you use are stored in a buffer. If you make a mistake during the editing and creation process, you can use the **undo** command to "back up" a single step or even multiple steps in the drawing process. To use this command, simply type **undo**↵ at the **Command:** prompt. Each time you type **undo**, AutoCAD will back up to the previous step. For example, if you make a mistake when adding a parametric dimension, the **undo** command will restore your model to the state it was in before adding the dimensions. You'll find that it is usually easier to "back up" steps in creating a Designer model, than to fix the model if you make a mistake.

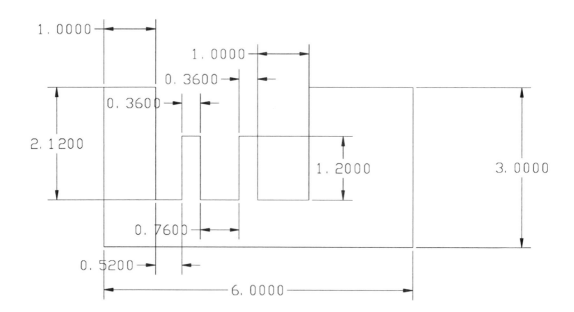

Figure 6-4 *Fully constrained profile with dimensions*

Step Three: Extruding to a 3-D Model

The completely defined profile will be extruded to form a 3-D solid part. You will use the **adextrude** command to complete this operation.

    Select: **Designer>Features>Extrude** *from the pull-down menu.*

    Complete the Designer **Extrusion** Box, specifying a **Blind** termination, and an extrusion distance of 3 units.

Part Viewing

Change to two viewports: one will be an isometric view, the other will be used to look at the part from the direction of the current sketch plane.

    Command: **vports**

    Save/Restore/Delete/Join/SIngle/?/2/<3>/4: **2**

    Horizontal/<Vertical>: ↵

    Now we will assign the view point for each viewport. The Designer **adpartview** command can be used to automatically view the part from the top, any side, bottom, isometric view, or from the current sketch plane.

    Activate the right View Port by clicking the mouse in that viewport.

    Select: **Designer>Part Viewing>Iso** *from the pull-down menu.*

    If you loaded the **AutoLisp** routines, **adbonus1** and **adbonus2** (see Chapter 4), then you can simply type in **2**↵ at the **command**: prompt to create two viewports.

Step Four: Creating a Sketch Plane

A **sketch plane** is a plane used for sketching profiles and paths. A sketch plane can be placed on a planer face or a work plane. The current active sketch plane is the plane on the front face of the part (where we created the original profile). The Designer **adskpln** command is used to move the sketch plane and to define the direction of its X- and Y-coordinates. Before you can drill a hole lengthwise through the part, you need to move the sketch plane to the surface that you are drilling from. Before you can drill a hole, though, you need to attach the current sketch plane to the right end of the part. Another profile could also be defined on this new sketch plane, to be used for adding additional 3-D features to the base part.

    Select: **Designer>Sketch>Sketch Plane** *from the pull-down menu.*

    Xy/Yz/Zx/Ucs/<Select work plane or planar face>: *Select P1 on Figure 6-5.*

    The end surface should be highlighted. Since *P1* is located on an edge common to two surfaces, Designer gives you the option of toggling between selected surfaces **<Next>.** If another surface is highlighted, you can toggle between surfaces by typing

N until you have selected the end surface. Type **A** to accept the selection when the proper surface is highlighted. ↵ completes the selection.

X/Y/Z/<Select work axis or straight edge>: *Select P2 on Figure 6-5. This will be the X axis for the new sketch plane.*

Rotate/<Accept>: *You can rotate the X-Y coordinate system on the new sketch plane 90° by typing* **R**. *Type* **A**↵ *to accept the coordinate system rotation.*

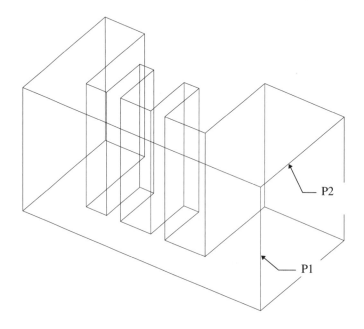

Figure 6-5 *Placing the sketch plane on the end of the part*

There is now a Sketch Plane on the end of the part. You can use the **Part Viewing** command to view the part through the current sketch plane.

Select: **Designer>Part Viewing>Sketch**

Your screen should look similar to the one shown in Figure 6-6, showing the part through the current sketch plane.

Step Five: Drilling Holes

Using the **adhole** command, drill a hole through the part. The holes are always drilled normal to the current active sketch plane. Since you moved the sketch plane to the right end of the part in the previous step, the **adhole** command will drill a hole through that surface.

Select: **Designer>Features>Hole...**

The Designer **Hole Dialogue** Box will appear.

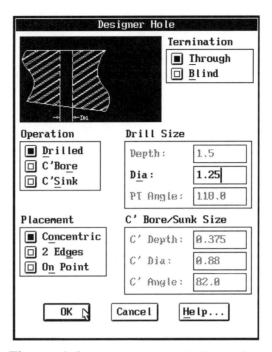

Figure 6-6 *Designer hole dialogue box*

Complete the box so that it looks like the one shown in Figure 6-6. You will drill a 1.25″ hole completely through the part from the right end. The hole will be located on the end surface by specifying a distance from the two edges.

Select **OK**.

Designer will now prompt you for the exact location of the hole.

Select first edge: *Select P4 in Figure 6-7.*

Select second edge: *Select P5.*

Select hole location: *Pick near the center of the box. (It doesn't matter how close to the center it is.)*

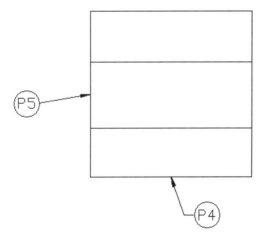

Figure 6-7 *Hole placement*

Distance from first edge: *2.0*

Distance from second edge: *1.5*

You should see a hole drilled entirely through the part. The isometric view of your part should look like the one shown in Figure 6-8.

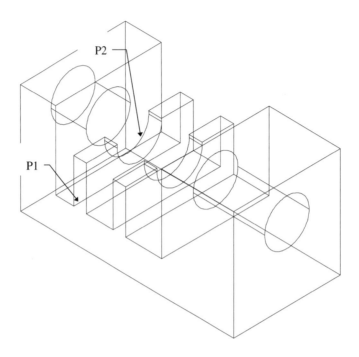

Figure 6-8 *Chain rivet extractor after hole is drilled through the part*

Step Six: Creating the Semicircles

The chain rivet extractor requires a 1.75 inch semicircular cutout on each of the two inner webs. The hole you just drilled through the part cut a semicircle with a 1.25 inch diameter. The new semicircle must be slightly larger than the 1.25 inch diameter hole which was drilled through the part. The **adhole** command can be used to "cut" a larger semicircle through each of the two webs. To do this, the hole is cut only a certain depth by using the **blind** termination option and specifying the exact depth to cut. Since the semicircle will be concentric to the 1.25 inch hole you previously created, the easiest way to locate this hole is to specify the **concentric** location option on the Designer Hole dialogue box.

Select: **Designer>Features>Hole...** *from the pull-down menus.*

Complete the Designer Hole dialogue box so that it looks like Figure 6-9. Note that the termination must be checked as **blind** and the placement must be specified as **concentric**.

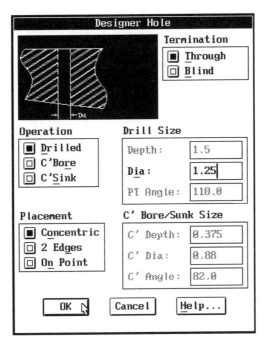

Figure 6-9 *Hole dialog box*

X/Y/Z/Ucs/Select work plane or planar face: *Select P1 to locate the hole on the same face as the current sketch plane as shown in Figure 6-8.*

Select concentric edge: *Pick point P2 on the semicircle.*

Work Features: Planes, Points, and Axes

So far, you've been able to create 3-D geometry simply by moving and attaching the sketch plane to different surfaces on your part. As long as a flat surface exists on the part, you can attach a sketch plane to that part for 3-D construction. However, many times you will be constructing a part with curved features, or you will need to attach a sketch plane somewhere "inside" the part. For these cases, you will need to use the work features of designer: **work planes, work axes,** or **work points**. The work features are either points, axes, or planes that can be located and attached parametrically to your model. They are construction features to aid you in building a parametric model. Since work features are not actually a solid feature of the part, they do not appear in drawings, and do not contribute to the mass properties of the part. You have the option of turning off the display of these construction aides.

Work points are parametric "points" which can be attached to a surface. They assist in locating holes and circular features. Work points do not appear in the final drawing of your model, but are useful when you need an "anchor" to locate a hole. Because work points are parametric, you locate them by defining parametric dimensions relative to features on the part, similar to defining a profile. Work points are displayed as three small orthogonal axes on your model, but do not show when creating a drawing.

Work axes are parametric centerlines which are located along the centerlines of curved surfaces in your model. They can be used to locate work planes and to locate new sketched features. Work axes appear as the centerline linetype and the display of work axes can be toggled off from the **Display** menu. They are useful when constructing features which need to be located at some distance or angle from a curved surface. Since work axes are parametric, they always move whenever the curved surface is edited or moved.

Work planes are defined as "infinite planes located in AutoCAD model space and associated with the part that was active at the time of their creation." Work planes are similar to sketch planes but serve a very different role in the modeling process. Work planes are used as construction aides and to define a parametric location for a sketch plane. They are used when it is not possible to attach a sketch plane directly to a flat surface of the part. Unlike sketch planes, work planes do not have coordinate axes. You can create an unlimited number of work planes associated with your active part, but you can only have **one** sketch plane active at a time. You can use the edges, planes, and vertices of the active part to define work planes. Work planes appear on a part as a planar rectangle lying on the work plane.

Work planes can be used for the following purposes:

- As a sketching plane for sketching new features
- To identify cutting planes for cross-sectional views in drawings
- To create an intermediate position upon which you can define other work planes
- For sketching new features with dimensions placed according to the edge view of the work plane
- As a boundary in a sketch for a new profile or path

There are two types of work planes: **parametric** and **nonparametric**. **Parametric** work planes are associated with a part's edge, surface, or other feature. The plane moves and changes with the part. **Nonparametric** work planes remain constant with a fixed location with respect to the part, because they do not have any geometric links to the part. Designer allows you to locate parametric work planes using 12 different combinations of constraints.

Workplane Constraint Options

The following figures will help you understand the different ways you can attach work planes to your part.

On Edge/Axis & On Edge/Axis

Note that you must first define work axes through the holes or circular features on your part. These axes are then used to locate the work plane.

Work Features: Planes, Points, and Axes 101

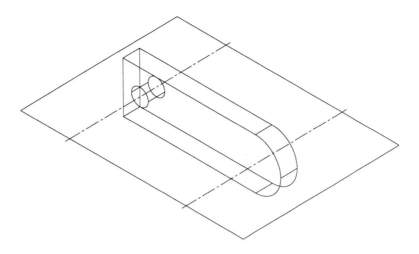

Figure 6-10 *Work plane through the hole axis and through the axis of curved surface*

On Edge/Axis & On Vertex

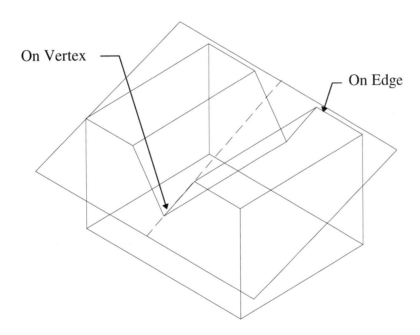

Figure 6-11 *Work plane through the front vertex and back edge of part*

On Edge/Axis & Tangent

Note that you must first define a work axis through the hole or circular feature that you are using to locate this work plane. This option can be used to drill a hole normal to a curved surface as shown in Figure 6-12.

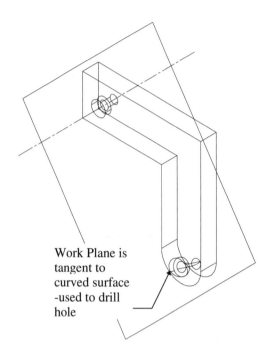

Figure 6-12 *Work plane located on the axis and tangent to curved surface*

On Edge/Axis & Planar Parallel

Note that you must first define a work axis through the hole or circular feature that you are using to locate this work plane.

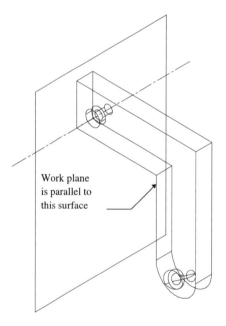

Figure 6-13 *Work plane through the axis of hole and parallel to a face of the part*

Work Features: Planes, Points, and Axes

On Edge/Axis & Planar Normal

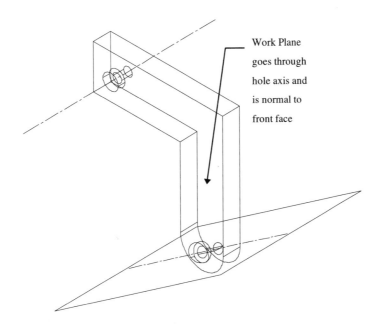

Figure 6-14 *Work plane goes through the axis of the hole and is normal to the plane of face*

On Edge/Axis & Planar Angle

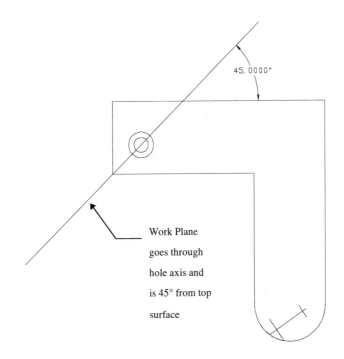

Figure 6-15 *Work plane goes through the axis of the hole and is at a specified angle to the top surface*

On Vertex & Planar Parallel

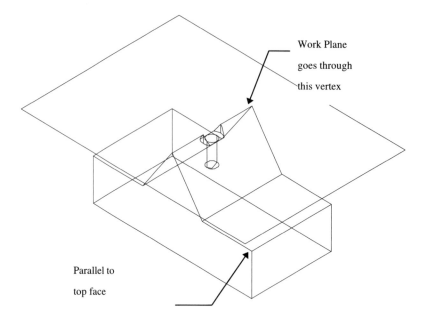

Figure 6-16 *Work plane goes through the vertex on top of part and is parallel with the top surface*

On Vertex & 3 Vertices

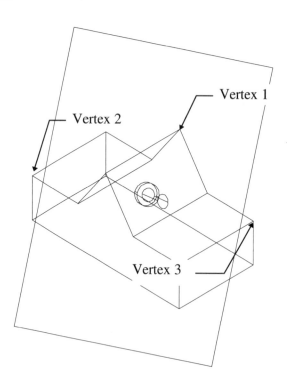

Figure 6-17 *Three vertices have been selected to locate work plane*

Work Features: Planes, Points, and Axes 105

Tangent & Planar Parallel

This option is useful when you need to locate a feature such as a hole on a curved surface. Because of the method Designer uses to define curved entities, you are not able to locate a feature on a curved surface unless you first specify the appropriate work plane.

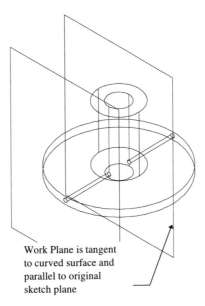

Figure 6-18 *Work plane is tangent to the curved plate and is located parallel to a work plane attached to the original sketch plane*

Tangent & Planar Normal

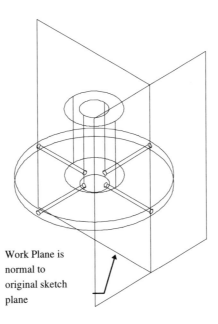

Figure 6-19 *The work plane is located tangent to the curved plate and normal to a work plane attached to the original sketch plane*

Step Seven: Creating a New Work Plane through the Center of the Part

The next step in constructing the chain rivet extractor is an operation to round the corners at each end of the part. The simplest way to do this operation is to construct an arc through the center of the part. This arc will then form the template to do a **revolved cut** operation. The revolved profile will actually cut or clip the corners of the part, thereby producing the rounded corners shown in Figure 6-1.

Since a sketch plane can only be attached to a planar surface, you cannot directly locate a sketch plane through the center of the chain rivet extractor. You first have to define a parametric work plane through the center of the part, and then attach a sketch plane to this work plane. The simplest way to construct this new sketch plane is to locate it along the centerline of drilled 1.25-inch hole in the chain rivet extractor. Therefore, you will define a work axis along the centerline of this hole. This work axis will then be used as a reference line to locate a work plane through the center of the part. Finally, a sketch plane will be attached to the new work plane, to be used as the active plane for constructing a curved surface of revolution.

To begin this construction process, create a **work axis** through the holes in the part.

Select: **Designer>Feature>Work Axis**

Select cylindrical face: *Select one of the holes.*

A work axis is now created and displayed as a center-line through the part.

Designer supports twelve options for locating work planes. These options are selected from the Designer **Work Plane** dialogue box. The work plane you will create is located parallel to the front face of the part, along the work axis you just created.

Select: **Designer>Feature>Work Plane...**

The Work Plane dialogue box appears.

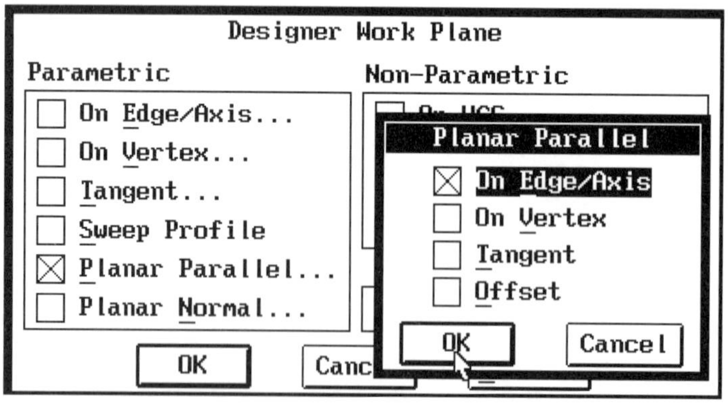

Figure 6-20 *Work plane dialogue box*

Select a **Planar Parallel** work plane that is **On Edge/Axis**

Designer will prompt you to select the location of the new work plane:

X/Y/Z/<Select work axis or straight edge>: *Select work axis created through the center of the circles.*

Xy/Yz/Zx/Ucs/<Select work plane or planar face>: *Pick P1 in Figure 6-21 to locate the new work plane parallel to the front face of the part.*

Designer gives you the option of toggling between selected surfaces using *<Next>*. If the wrong surface is highlighted, you can toggle between surfaces by typing **N**.

The work plane is now created and displayed as a square plane through the part. Your model should look like Figure 6-22.

Step Eight: Creating a Sketch Plane on a Work Plane

Select: **Designer>Sketch>Sketch Plane** *from the pull-down menus.*

Designer will prompt you for the location of the sketch plane:

Xy/Yz/Zx/Ucs/<Select work plane or planar face>: *Select the work plane you just created.*

X/Y/Z<Select work axis or straight edge>: *Select P1(the work axis).*

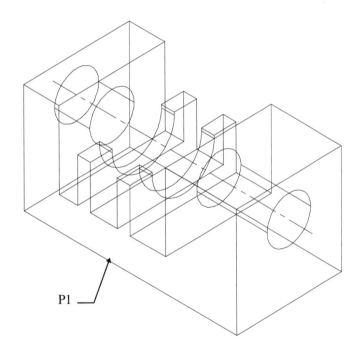

Figure 6-21 *Placement of the work plane*

Rotate/<Accept>: **R** *(Note: You may have to rotate more than once to get the proper alignment.)*

Rotate/<Accept>: ↵

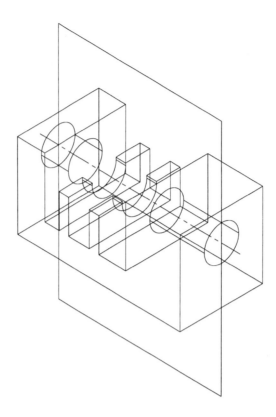

Figure 6-22 *New work plane through the center of the part*

Change the Left Viewport to the Sketch plane view

Select the left viewport.

Select: **Designer>Part Viewing>Sketch**

The Left Viewport now displays the active sketch plane.

Step Nine: Creating a Curved "Cutting" Profile on the Sketch Plane

A semicircular profile will be used as a "template" for rounding the corners of the chain rivet extractor. By revolving this profile around an axis along the center of the part, you can create equally rounded corners.

Sketch a horizontal line in the center of the part on the sketch plane.

Select: **Draw>Line>Segments**

Draw a line across the part.

Sketch an arc across the sketch plane from the endpoints of the line.

Select: **Draw>Arc>Start, End, Dir**

Center/<Start point>: *Pick an endpoint of the line. (The arc does not have to connect "exactly" with the line; just get the points close.)*

Center/End/<Second point>: *Pick the other endpoint.*

Angle/Direction/Radius/<Center point>: **d**

Direction from start point: *Drag the mouse to make the angle of the arc cross the corners of the part. ↵ completes the operation. The completed sketch should look similar to the one shown in Figure 6-23.*

Next, you will create a profile of the new sketch by adding dimensions to it.

Select: **Designer>Sketch>Profile**

Select objects: *Select some point on the sketch.*

↵ *to complete the selection.*

Designer will generate the message:

```
Solved under constrained sketch requiring 4 dimensions /
constraints.
```

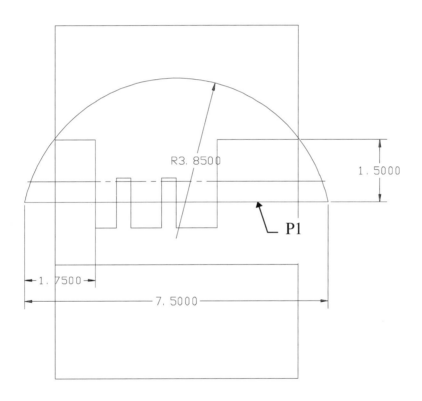

Figure 6-23 *Semicircular profile for revolve operation*

To complete the profile, you need to specify the radius of the arc, the length of the horizontal baseline, and the X and Y location of the arc's centerpoint. Use the **adpardim** command to add dimensions to the new sketch.

Select: **Designer>Sketch>Add Dimension**

Dimension the arc according to the values shown in the above figure. The sketch should be fully constrained before continuing.

Step Ten: Revolve the New Profile to Round the Corners of the Part

The semicircular profile you created in the previous step will be used as a "cookie cutter" to round the corners of the chain rivet extractor. The axis of revolution will be the horizontal baseline, which is located along the center of the part. As the profile is revolved 360° around this axis, it will clip the corners using the Designer "cut" operation. At the **command**: prompt, type **adrevolve** ↵ or using the pull-down menus:

Select: **Designer>Features>Revolve...**

The Designer **Revolve** dialogue box will appear. Edit the dialogue box to match the settings in Figure 6.24. You will perform an **intersecting** revolution with **full** termination. This will revolve the sketch 360 degrees around the axis you choose, cutting any material off the part that is crosses.

The different revolve options are discussed below.

Termination		Determines how the revolution is ended.
•	**By angle**	Revolves the profile to the specified angle.
•	**Mid Plane**	Revolves the profile equally in both directions, terminating at the specified overall angle.
•	**To Plane**	Defines the specified planar face or work plane to end the revolve operation.
•	**Full**	Revolves the profile 360 degrees.
Operation		Determines the Boolean operation of the revolution.
•	**Base**	Adds material, creating the first feature in a part.
•	**Cut**	Selects the type of cut to remove material from the active part.
•	**Join**	Adds material to the active part.
•	**Intersect**	Creates a new feature from the shared volume of the existing part and the revolved feature.
Size		This is the angle of revolution when specifying a **By Angle** termination.

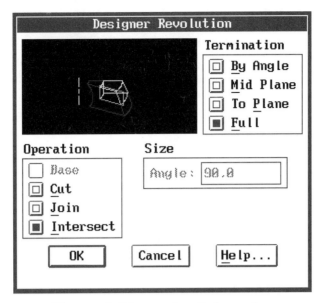

Figure 6-24 *Revolve dialogue box*

Click the **OK** button when you are finished. Designer will prompt you to select the axis of revolution. This axis must be one of the lines in the active profile.

Select axis of revolution: *Select the horizontal line in the new sketch (P1 in Figure 6-23).*

This operation may require a short wait, depending upon the speed of your computer. The corners are cut off and rounded, creating the desired result. The 3-D part is now complete. It should look similar to the figure below.

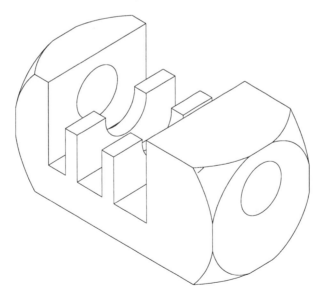

End of Chapter Summary

Using Designer work planes, work axes, and work points, you were able to create a complex 3-D solid model. This process was analogous to the engineering design process.

112 Advanced 3-D Construction: A Chain Rivet Extractor

You started with a basic profile and extruded that profile to create a solid "base" part. The 3-D construction aides were then used to refine this part by adding other profiles to various surfaces and features on the part. Using the Boolean operations of cut, join, and intersect, you were then able to remove and/or add material to the base part to create the complex 3-D geometry shown in the figure on page 111. Using Designer's revolve features you were able to revolve a profile about an axis, creating a part with radial symmetry.

Exercises

Using Designer, construct the following objects. Using the Designer **Create Drawing**, create a layout with three primary orthographic views and an isometric view similar to the ones shown below. Remember, if you get stuck on a particular operation, use the **Undo** feature of AutoCAD to "back up" one or more operations.

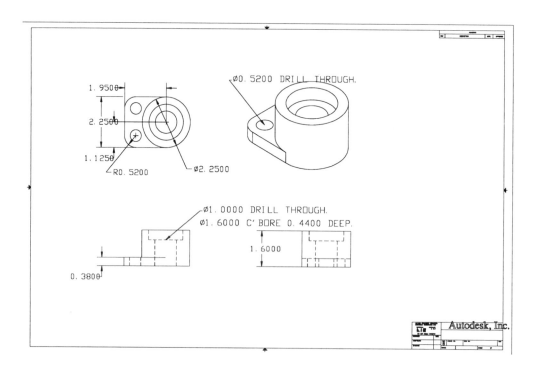

Ex 6-1

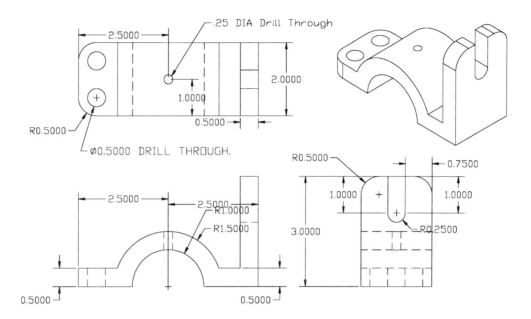

Ex 6-2

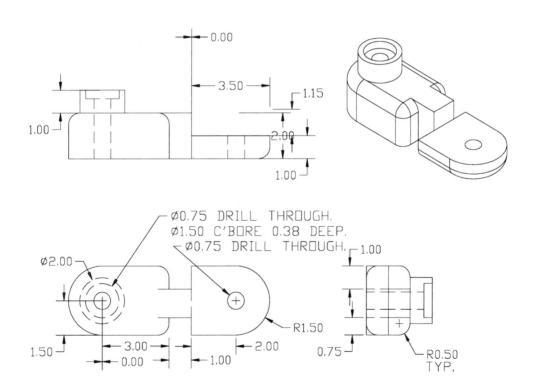

Ex 6-3

114 Advanced 3-D Construction: A Chain Rivet Extractor

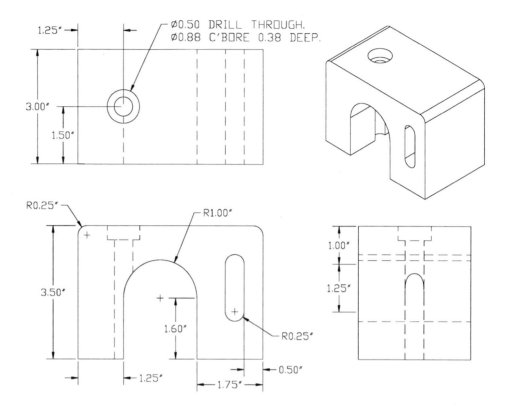

Ex 6-4

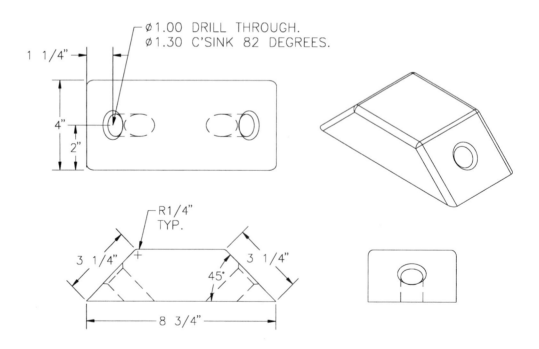

Ex 6-5

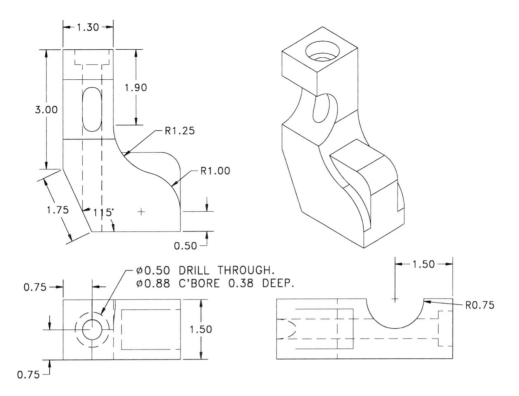

Ex 6-6

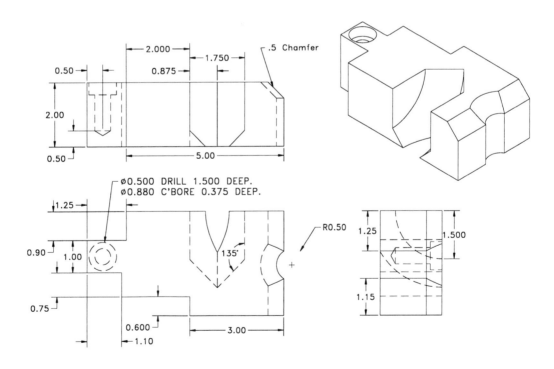

Ex 6-7

116 Advanced 3-D Construction: A Chain Rivet Extractor

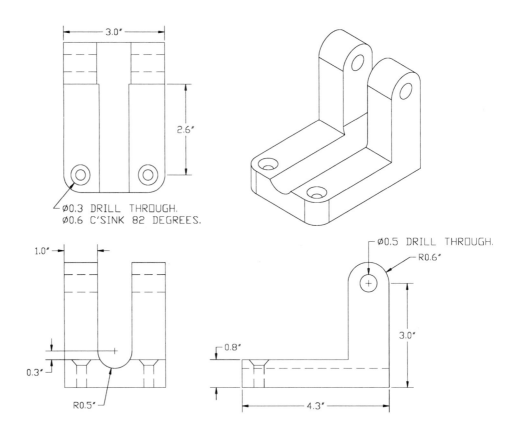

Ex 6-8

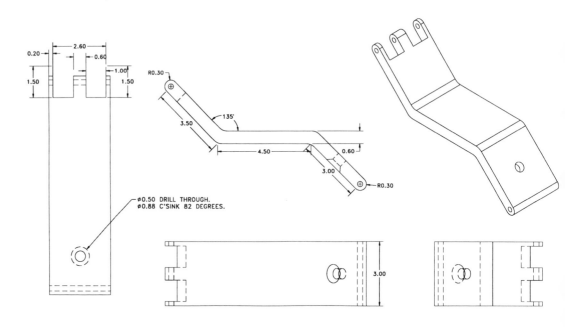

Ex 6-9

Chapter 7

Using 3-D Sweeps and Basic Parametric Equations

When you have completed this lesson you will be able to:

1. **Create a 3-D "Swept" solid**
2. **Understand how to define a sweep path**
3. **Use a "sweep profile" work plane**
4. **Understand basic parametric equations and how to use global parameters to define part geometry**

Introduction

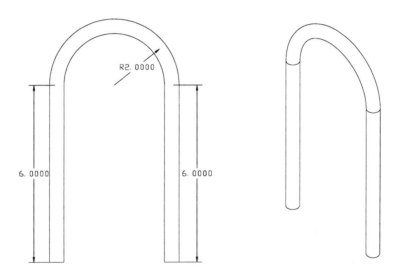

Figure 7-1 *Sweep model of a U bolt*

This lesson illustrates how to use the three-dimensional **sweep** features of Designer to create a solid model similar to the U bolt shown above. A **swept** model is created when a 2-D profile is swept along a 3-D path. The U bolt shown in Figure 7-1 was created by defining a "U-shaped" path in 3-D space. A circular profile was then created at the endpoint of this path and normal to the path. The profile was then swept along the path to create the solid model.

This lesson also illustrates the important concept of **global parameters,** which are variables that can be used in mathematical equations to define the geometry and relate geometrical elements to each other. The geometry of the Designer models you've created so far has been defined by simple numerical values which represent sizes, shapes, etc. An engineering design problem, though, will usually require mathematical relationships between the various geometrical elements of the model. For example, if you are designing a bearing sleeve and shaft assembly, the shaft diameter must be defined so that it is smaller than the hole diameter by a given amount. Designer has the ability to define geometry in terms of mathematical relationships, such as **shaftdiam = holediam - clearance**, where **clearance** is the clearance or "gap" between the hole and shaft. Global parameters are important when creating assembly models. Using global parameters, the geometry of a part can be defined in terms of mating parts. Global parameters can therefore be used to link various parts in an assembly, producing an unambiguous and geometrically consistent model. In this lesson you will use global parameters to define the geometry of the U bolt. These same global parameters will then be used in following lesson, to geometrically link the U bolt to a clamp assembly.

Defining Global Parameters

Prior to creating the sweep solid, you will define two global parameters, **boltlen** and **arcrad**. These parameters will be used to define the geometry and size of the U bolt. By using global parameters rather than numeric values to define dimensions, you can create a model which can be easily modified later on. Global parameters also allow you to link this part to other parts, forming an assembly. Global parameters can be used as variables in an equation, thereby allowing you to define the model geometry mathematically. For example, equations of stress and strain can be used in parametric equations to define the size of a part in terms of it's material properties. These parametric equations can be easily edited and modified, thereby directly modifying the geometry of the model.

The **adparam** command can be used to create, delete, list, import, or export global parameters. To execute this command, type **adparam**↵ at the **Command**: prompt, or use the Designer pull-down menus:

Select **Designer>Parameters>Create** from the pull-down menus.

Enter equation: **boltlen=6.**↵ *This will create a new global parameter named "boltlen" and assign a value of 6.0 to this parameter. Because the parameter is "global," it is available to define the geometry of all Designer parts in your drawing database.*

Designer will respond with:

Parameter "boltlen" created: current value = =6

Enter equation: **arcrad=2.**↵ *This will create a new global parameter named "arcrad."*

Parameter "arcrad" created: current value = =2

Enter equation: ↵ *This will return you to the **adpardim** prompt:*

Create/Delete/List/Import/Export/<eXit>: **L**↵ *Type* **L** *to list the parameters you just created. Designer will show all the parameters in a table format.*

	Parameter Name	Definitions
1)	boltlen	=6
2)	arcrad	=2

Create/Delete/List/Import/Export/<eXit>: *X↵ Type X to exit.*

When defining global parameters, you can assign a numeric value to the parameter, such as **boltlen**, or you can use mathematical equations to define the parameter. The parameter, **arcrad**, was defined as a function of **boltlen**, rather than by assigning a numerical value. By using equations or mathematical relationships to define these parameters, you are able to more easily modify your model and still maintain basic geometric consistency between the various elements of the model. The geometry of the model can be changed by either modifying the global equations, or by assigning new values to the global parameters. Therefore, parametric equations allow a design engineer to maintain fundamental geometric relationships in the model based upon principles of engineering mathematics, even as the model is edited.

Building Sweeps

Creating a sweep is analogous to creating a part using extrusion techniques. The process closely parallels the process of solving an engineering design problem. Solving a design problem requires a sequential methodology. To build a sweep feature, you follow these five steps:

1. **Sketch a "path."** This is similar to creating the "rough" sketch of a 2-D profile for an extrusion part. The initial path is not drawn according to exact dimensions or geometric constraints. Parametric dimensions are added to the path in the same way you add them to the 2-D sketch profile for an extrusion model.

2. **Create a sweep work plane.** Once you have defined the sweep path, you will locate a work plane normal to one end of the path.

3. **Create a sketch plane.** A sketch plane is attached to the sweep work plane. This sketch plane is then used to construct the 2-D profile geometry which will be used to define the sweep cross section.

4. **Create a profile.** A 2-D "rough" sketch is created on the new sketch plane. Parametric dimensions and geometric constraints are used to turn this sketch into a fully constrained profile the same way you do for an extrusion model.

5. **Create the sweep.** The final step is to sweep the 2-D cross section profile along the path you created in the first step.

Step One: Create a Sweep Path

Draw a sketch of the sweep path

Begin this project by creating a "rough" sketch of the sweep path. You may use most of the regular AutoCAD drawing and editing features such as line, circle, arcs, or polylines. At this point you are not concerned about exact dimensions and locations. The easiest way to draw your sketch is to use an AutoCAD **polyline** (**pline**). Draw the path so it looks similar to the one shown in Figure 7-2.

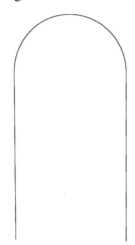

Figure 7-2 *Sketch profile of sweep path*

Turn the sketch into a constrained sweep path

Designer's **adpath** command will be used to clean up the sketch in the same way the **adprofile** command is used to clean up an extrusion sketch. After sketching the path, the **adpath** command will solve the sketch and apply geometric constraints. Lines will be snapped to horizontal or vertical, arcs will be constrained as tangent to lines, etc. Type **adpath**↵ at the **Command:** prompt or use the Designer pull-down menu:

Select: **Designer>Sketch>Path** *from the pull-down menus*

Select objects for sketch: *Select all of the 2-D geometry. (You can 'window' the entire sketch. If you used a polyline, pick one part of the line.)*

Select start point of path: *Select near the left endpoint of the vertical line.*

Designer will generate the message:

Solved under constrained sketch requiring 3 dimensions/constraints.

Adpath works much like **adprofile** except that it will allow use of an open sketch. **Adpath** works exclusively on sweep paths. You should not use the **adprofile** command to create a sweep path.

Parametric dimensions

Parametric dimensions and constraints are added to a sweep path in the same way they are added to a Designer profile. For this example, though, you will use global parameters to define the geometry instead of numeric dimensions as you've done in previous problems. The two global parameters you defined in the first part of this example will be used to determine the geometry of the U bolt. Since these parameters are *global*, they can also be used to define the geometry of the mating parts which you'll create in the next lesson.

Change the way dimensions are displayed

Prior to using parametric relationships to define the geometry, you will need to change the default dimension viewing mode. When dimensioning a sketch, Designer shows the numeric values of all dimensions by default. When using parametric equations to define the geometry, you need to see the parameter names that Designer associates with the geometry. The following three options for dimension display are available. Figure 7-3 illustrates the differences between these three dimension display options.

- **Parameters**   This option shows only the dimension parameter name. When Designer solves the sketch, it automatically assigns names to all dimensions, beginning with *d0* and incrementing the integer as for each geometric entity.

- **Equations**   This option shows the equation for dimensions that have been defined with a parametric equation.

- **Numeric**   This option shows only the current numeric value. This is the default option when creating a new model.

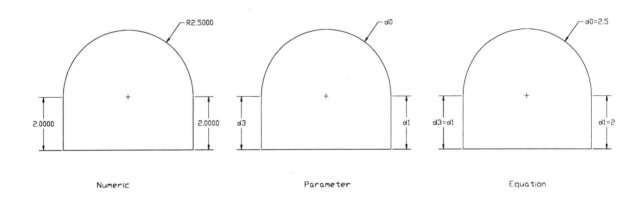

Figure 7-3 *Designer's dimension display options*

The default dimension display mode can be changed by the **addimdsp** command. To change the dimension display mode to equations (which show the parameter names) type **addimdsp**↵ at the **Command:** prompt, or use the pull-down menus:

Select: **Designer>Display>Dim Display**

Parameters/Equations/<Numeric>: **E** ↵ *Type* **E** *to toggle to the Equation dimension display mode.*

Designer will now display the parameter names and any equations used to define the geometry.

Add parametric dimensions to the sweep path

The **adpardim** command will be used to add parametric dimensions to the path. This command is used in much the same way as in previous lessons, except you will not use numeric values to define the dimensions. Instead, the two global parameters, **arcrad** and **boltlen**, will be used to define the length and radius of the U bolt path. From the pull-down menus:

Select: **Designer>Sketch>Add Dimensions**

Select first item: *Pick near the midpoint of one of the vertical lines.*

Undo/Hor/Ver/Align/Par/Dim value<XX.XX>: =**boltlen**↵ *Instead of typing a numeric value for this dimension, you will type the = sign followed by the global parameter name.*

Designer will then assign the current value for **boltlen** to this dimension. Notice that the equation and parameter name are shown on your sketch, since you modified the dimension display in the previous step. Designer will respond with the following message:

`Solved underconstrained sketch requiring 2 dimensions/constraints.`

Select first item: *Pick any point on the arc.*

Undo/Dimension value<XX.XX>: =**arcrad**↵ *Again, type an = sign followed by the global parameter name to assign the current value of arcrad to this radius.*

Repeat this process for the remaining vertical line, assigning it a value of **boltlen**. When completed, your sketch should look like the one shown in Figure 7-4. Notice how Designer assigns variable names *d0 to d3* for the various geometric entities defining the path. The variable names are incremented in the order you initially constructed the sketch. For example, the sketch in Figure 7-4 was constructed starting with the left vertical line and drawing the remaining lines clockwise. Had you drawn your sketch in the reverse order (starting with the right vertical line), the variable names would be different. If you delete a dimension or modify the sketch, the variable names may change from the ones shown in Figure 7-4. Since you've toggled the dimension display mode to show equations, the full parametric equations will be displayed. If you switch back to a numeric display, then your sketch will only show the current values of **arcrad** and **boltlen** when displaying dimensions.

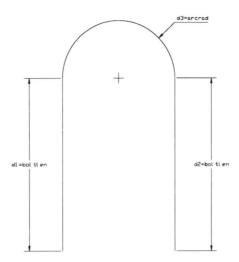

Figure 7-4 *Fully dimensioned and constrained sweep path*

Step Two: Create a sweep work plane

Now that you've defined the path for the sweep, you will have to locate the sweep profile. Before you can construct the sweep profile, you need to define a sketch plane at one end of the sweep path and normal to the path. Designer has a special option in the **Work Plane** dialogue box specifically for locating a selectable start point on the sweep path.

To construct this work plane, use the pull-down menus:

Designer>Features>Work Plane...

Check the **Sweep Profile** box in the **Work Plane** dialogue box. Designer will prompt you to:

Select an item in the path: *Pick anywhere on the left vertical line of the sweep profile.*

Complete the **Work Plane** dialogue box as shown in Figure 7-5.

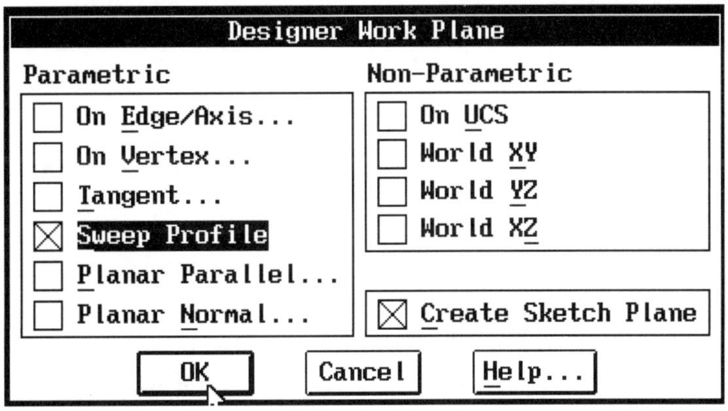

Figure 7-5 *Designer Work Plane dialogue box for creating sweep profiles*

The work plane will be attached normal to the path as shown in Figure 7-6.

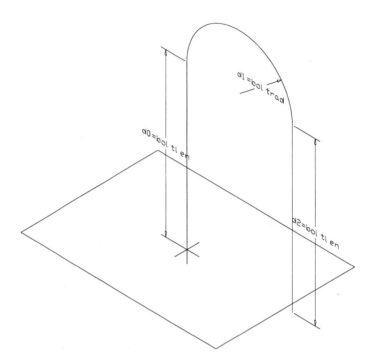

Figure 7-6 *Sweep work plane attached to sweep profile*

Step Three: Create a sketch plane

Once you've created a Sweep Profile work plane, you set the sketch plane on it. You can use the **adskpln** command and select the work plane you just created. From the pull-down menus:

   Select: **Designer>Sketch>Sketch Plane**

As an alternative, you can use the **Create Sketch Plane** option in the Designer **Work Plane** dialogue box when creating the Sweep Profile work plane. This option automatically attaches the sketch plane to the work plane you are creating, thereby combining two steps into one.

Step Four: Create a profile

You will now draw a circle, which forms the basis for a Designer profile to be swept along the previously defined path. Since this circle is to be centered on the sketch path, you will need to define three parametric dimensions before it is fully defined and constrained. In addition to specifying the diameter of the circle, you need to locate the X- and Y-coordinates of the centerpoint.

Before drawing the circle and adding parametric dimensions, you should change the view of the model to the current sketch plane. Use the **adpartview** command to select the sketch plane as the current view. Type **adpartview**↵ at the **Command**: prompt and type **Sketch** for the part viewing option. You can also use the pull-down menus:

   Designer>Part Viewing>Sketch

If you loaded the **adbonus2.lsp** (see Chapter 3) routines, you can type **3↵** to show the part from three separate viewpoints. You may need to use the AutoCAD zoom command before the image is large enough to construct the circle.

If You're New to AutoCAD: Zoom Command

The **Zoom** command is used to enlarge or reduce the display of your drawing on the screen. **Zoom** does not change the size of your model or drawing, it only changes how large the image is on the screen. Sometimes when creating small details or parts in a Designer model, you need to enlarge a specific area of the drawing in order to edit or create the detail. The easiest way to do a zoom is to simply type **zoom↵** at the **Command:** prompt.

AutoCAD will respond with several options:

All/Center/Dynamic/Extents/Left/Previous/Vmax/Window/<Scale(X/XP)>:

The options that you will use most often with Designer are **Window, All,** and **Previous.** The **zoom>window** option allows you to drag an imaginary window around some area of your screen. After selecting the second corner of the window, AutoCAD will enlarge the window area to fill the full screen or viewport. The **zoom>previous** option will return your screen to the previous size before executing a zoom command. The **zoom>all** option will automatically zoom the screen image so that the entire model fits within the screen or viewport.

Use an AutoCAD **circle** command to draw a circle centered over the sweep path. You do not have to draw it exactly, since you will constrain and add parametric dimensions to the circle in the next step. Your completed sketch should look similar to the one shown in Figure 7-7.

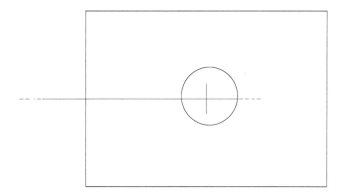

Figure 7-7 *Sweep profile viewed from the active sketch plane*

Once the circle is sketched, use the **adprofile** command to create a Designer 2-D profile from the circular sketch.

Define a new global parameter

Since you are using parametric equations and global parameters to constrain and define this model, you will create a new global parameter to be used as the diameter of the U bolt. This parameter will be called **boltdia** and will be used in the next lesson as a basis for defining a hole diameter. **Boltdia** must be created and assigned a value before you can use it to dimension the circle. Use the **adparam** command to create a new global parameter. From the pull-down menus:

    Select **Designer>Parameters>Create**

    Enter equation: **boltdia=.5**↵ *This will create a new global parameter named "boltdia" and assign a value of 0.5 to this parameter.*

      Designer will respond with:

Parameter "boltdia" created: current value = =0.5

    Enter equation: ↵ *This will return you to the **adpardim** prompt.*

      To see a complete listing of all the current global parameters, use the **List** option of the **adpardim** command.

    Create/Delete/List/Import/Export/<eXit>: **L**↵ *Type L to list the parameters you just created. Designer will show all the parameters in a table format.*

	Parameter Name	Definitions
1)	boltlen	=6
2)	arcrad	=2
3)	boltdia	=0.5

    Create/Delete/List/Import/Export/<eXit>: **X**↵ *Type X to exit.*

Add parametric dimensions to the sketch

The next step is to use the **adpardim** command to constrain and dimension this profile. You will need to add three dimensions: the diameter of the circle and the X and Y location of the circle's centerpoint. You may need to zoom the circle large before you can add parametric dimensions.

    Select first item: ↵ *Select a point on the circle.*

    Select second item or place dimension: ↵ *Select a point outside the circle.*

    Undo/Dimension value (#): =**boltdia**↵ *The circle will be given a diameter of 0.5 units, which is the current value of the global parameter, "boltdia."*

      Repeat this command to dimension the centerpoint of the circle.

    Select first item: *Pick the circle again.*

Select second item or place dimension: *Select one of the vertical cross hairs on the sweep profile*

Undo/Hor/Ver/Align/Par/Dim value<XX.XX>: **H↵** *If a horizontal dimension is not displayed, type* **H↵** *to specify a horizontal dimension. Type a value of 0 to locate the horizontal position of the circle's centerpoint on the sweep profile.*

Select first item: *Pick the circle again.*

Select second item or place dimension: *Select one of the horizontal cross hairs on the sweep profile.*

Undo/Hor/Ver/Align/Par/Dim value<XX.XX>: **V↵** *If a vertical dimension is not displayed, type* **V↵** *to specify a vertical dimension. Type a value of 0 to locate the vertical position of the circle's centerpoint on the sweep profile.*

`Solved fully constrained sketch.`

The completed profile should look like the one shown in Figure 7-8 (shown from the current sketch plane). To see how this profile is attached to the sweep path, view it from an **isometric** option using the **adpartview** command discussed above. Your screen should look similar to Figure 7-9.

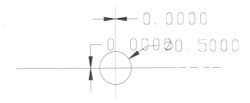

Figure 7-8 *Fully constrained sweep profile from sketch plane*

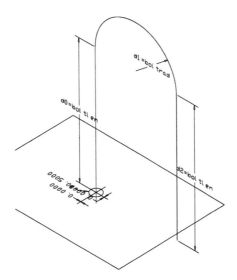

Figure 7-9 *Fully constrained sweep profile seen from an isometric viewpoint*

128 Using 3-D Sweeps and Basic Parametric Equations

Step Five: Create the sweep

Once the profile is fully defined, you are ready to complete the construction by executing the **adsweep** command. You can type this command at the prompt, or use the pull-down menus.

> Select: **Designer>Features>Sweep** *from the pull-down menus.*
>
> Select sweep path: *Select a point on the previously defined sweep path.*
>
> Select sweep cross section profile: *Select any point on the circle.*
>
> Parallel/<Normal>: **N↵** *This option will create a sweep with a profile normal to the sweep path. The parallel option will create a sweep maintaining a profile parallel to the profile sketch plane.*

Designer will create a complete swept solid of the U bolt. Your model should look like the one shown in Figure 7-10 when complete.

Editing Global Parameters

The power of global parameters in a Designer model becomes obvious when you edit the parameters to modify the geometry of the model. Since global parameters determine geometric relationships between different elements in a model or even across a set of AutoCAD drawings, they provide a very convenient way of simultaneously modifying all related elements of the model. Rather than edit and modify individual parametric dimensions as you've done previously, you simply edit the parametric equations or global parameter values, and all related geometry is automatically modified to reflect those changes.

The simplest way to edit global parameters is to use the **adparam** command and re-enter the value of the global parameter or parametric equation using the **Create** option. To illustrate how easily you can modify a Designer model by editing the global parameters, you will modify the value of *arcrad* and thereby change the U bolt model.

> Select **Designer>Parameters>Create** *from the pull-down menus.*
>
> Enter equation: **arcrad=3↵** *This will assign a new value to the existing global parameter "arcrad," replacing the current 2.0 value.*
>
> Designer will respond with:

```
Parameter "arcrad" created: current value = =3.0
```

> Enter equation: ↵ *This will return you to the **adpardim** prompt.*

Since Designer does not automatically update the geometry of the model every time you change a dimension value, you need to type **adupdate↵** to update all geometry reflecting the new value of **arcrad**.

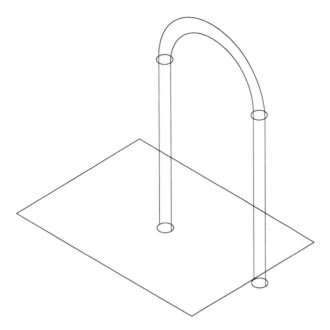

Figure 7-10 *Complete "U bolt" sweep model*

Finally, be sure to save your U bolt model in a file called **ubolt.dwg**. You will use this file as part of a designer assembly model in the following chapter.

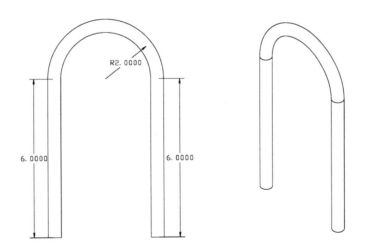

Figure 7-11 *Complete U bolt model showing dimensions*

End of Chapter Summary

You have defined global parameters which were used in parametric equations to define the geometry of a U bolt. The U bolt was constructed using Designer's sweep features. Since the geometry was completely dimensioned using three global parameters, you can

130 Using 3-D Sweeps and Basic Parametric Equations

then use these parameters as the basis for defining a clamp and nuts, as part of an assembly model. By using parameters, rather than numeric values, a design engineer has much greater control over the modification and editing of the model. In the next lesson you will create a complete assembly model by combining this U bolt with parametrically defined nuts and clamp.

Exercises

Use parametric equations to create the following solid models, and to define the dimensions in terms of the global parameters listed with each problem.

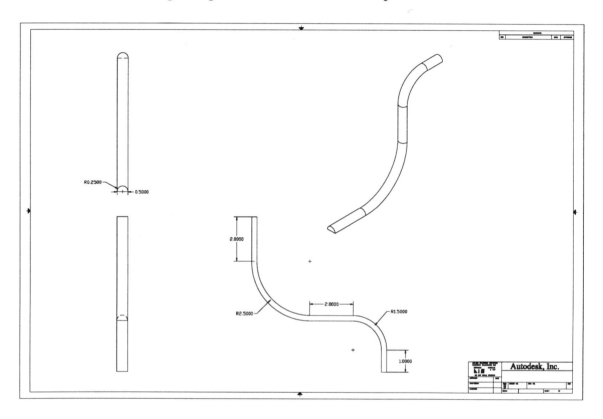

Ex 7-1. Create the above sweep profile using the sweep path shown at the top of page 136. Do not use numeric values to define the parametric dimensions, but create parametric equations, defining the sweep radii in terms of a global parametric variable.

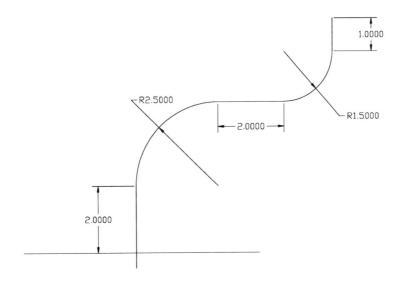

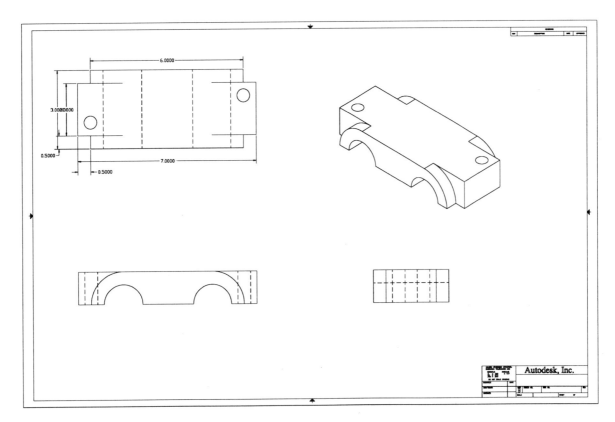

Ex 7-2. Use parametric equations to define the hole diameters in terms of the body size of the above part.

132 Using 3-D Sweeps and Basic Parametric Equations

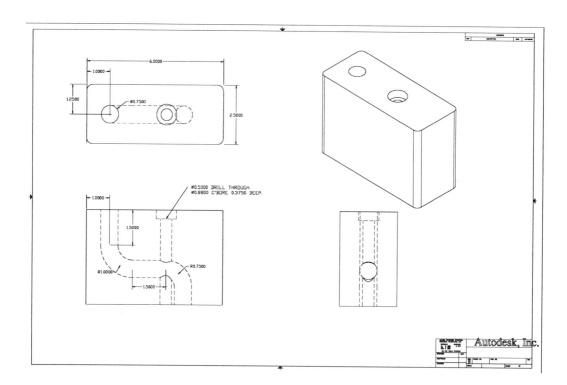

Ex 7-3. Use a sweep operation to cut the curved hole through the block.

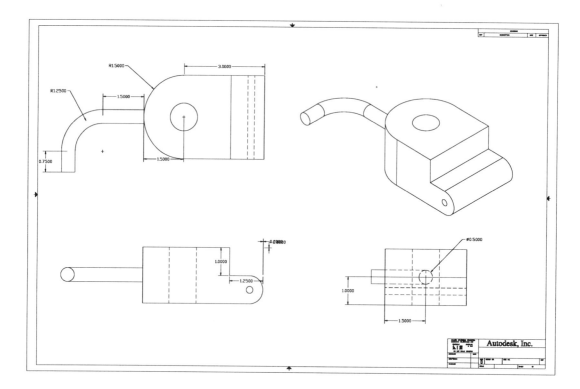

Ex 7-4. Create the part using parametric equations to define the geometry. Use a sweep to create the curved piece.

Chapter 8

Assembly Modeling Using Parametric Relationships

When you have completed this lesson you will be able to:

1. Create assembly models
2. Link "parts" together in an assembly model using global parameters
3. Import and export parametric files to define and edit model geometry
4. Have a better understanding of work axes and work planes

Introduction

In the previous chapter you created a U bolt using global parameters to define the model geometry. These global parameters can be used to define other "parts" in your model, thereby creating an assembly model. Using global parameters instead of numeric values has the advantage of assuring that the mating parts of your assembly will always fit together. In this exercise you will start with the U bolt model previously created. A mating clamp piece will be created using the same global parameters you used to define the U bolt geometry. Because each part of the assembly was defined using the same parameters, the mating parts will always have a correct "fit" even when making changes to the model geometry. When you finish this exercise, you will have a U bolt/clamp assembly similar to the one shown below.

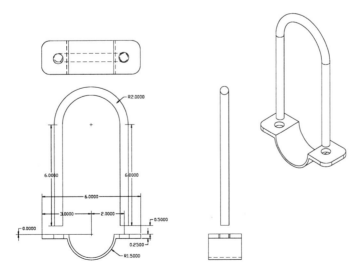

Figure 8-1 *U bolt clamp assembly*

134 Assembly Modeling Using Parametric Relationships

Step One: Create a Sketch Plane through the Axes of the U Bolt

You will begin this exercise by opening the file **ubolt.dwg**, which was created in the previous exercise. Since the U bolt geometry was defined using global variables such as **boltlen, arcrad,** and **boltdia**, these same variables can be used to define the geometry of the clamp piece that will attach to the U bolt.

Before constructing the clamp profile, you need to create a new sketch plane which intersects the axis of the U bolt arms. This sketch plane will allow you to define the clamp profile, and to ensure that the clamp will be placed symmetrically along the axis of the U bolt. The easiest way to create such a sketch plane is to attach a work plane to both axes of the U bolt.

Before you can attach a work plane, you must create work axes through the two arms of the U bolt. Use the Designer **adworkaxis** command. From the pull-down menus

Select **Designer>Features>Work Axis**

Select cylindrical face: *Select any point on the cylindrical arm of the U bolt.*

Repeat this command for the other cylinder. Designer should create a centerline along the axis of each cylinder.

Use the Designer **adworkpln** command to attach a work plane to each of the U bolt shaft axes. From the pull-down menus:

Select **Designer>Features>Work Plane...***You will see the Designer Work Plane dialogue box.*

Be sure to check the **Create Sketch Plane** box in the **Designer Work Plane** dialogue box to automatically attach the new sketch plane to this work plane. If you forget to check this box, then you'll need to attach a sketch plane to this work plane. After completing the dialogue box as shown in the figure below, click the **OK** button.

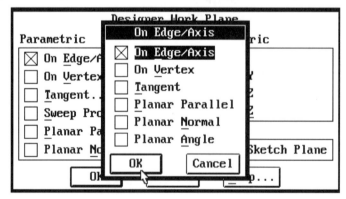

Figure 8-2 *Designer Work Plane dialogue box (axis/axis)*

Designer will prompt you to select the axis. Select each work axis you previously created and a work/sketch plane will be automatically created between these two axis. Your model should look similar to the one shown in Figure 8-3.

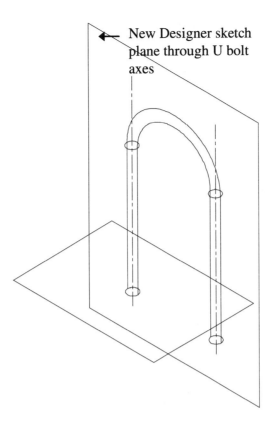

Figure 8-3 *Sketch/work plane through U bolt axes*

Step Two: Create a Profile of the Clamp Piece

You will start the clamp model like you've begun previous Designer models. You begin with a rough sketch, create a designer profile from the sketch, add parametric dimensions, and finally extrude the profile. What makes this model different from the previous ones is that you have already created part of the model in the previous lesson. To assure a proper fit between the clamp and the previously created U bolt, you will use the same global parameters to define the parametric dimensions of both parts.

View the model from the active sketch plane. Use the AutoCAD **adpartview** command to switch to this view:

Select **Designer>Part Viewing>Sketch** from the pull-down menus.

Using standard AutoCAD drawing commands (line, arc, or polyline) create a sketch similar to the one shown in Figure 8-4. You may find the construction easier if you first zoom in on the region you are using to draw.

136 Assembly Modeling Using Parametric Relationships

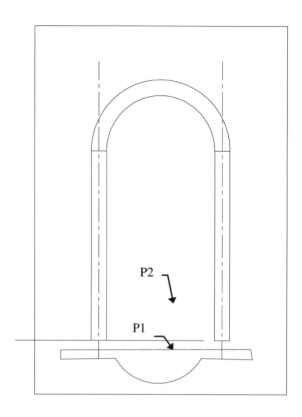

Figure 8-4 *Sketch profile of clamp piece*

Use **Designer>Display>Dim Display** to change the display mode. *At the prompt, type an* **E**. *This command will display all of your dimensions as parametric equations, rather than as the default of numbers.*

Parameters/Equations/<Numeric>: *E*↵

REMEMBER: **Parameters** shows only the dimension parameter name. **Equations** shows the equation that defines the dimension. **Numeric** shows only the current numeric value of that dimension.

Use the **Designer>Sketch>Profile** to create a profile from this sketch. Designer will "clean up" your sketch and respond with:

```
Solved under constrained sketch requiring 7
dimensions/constraints.
```

Use **Designer>Sketch>Add Dimension** to add the parametric dimensions needed to define the profile geometry.

Select first item: *Select P1 in Figure 8-4.*

Select second item or place dimension: *Pick a point somewhere above the line at P2 in Figure 8-4.*

Undo/Hor/Ver/Align/Par/Dimension value <##.##>: **=2*(arcrad+boltdia+.5)**↵
Instead of using a numerical value to define the length of this line, you will use a parametric equation and global parameters to define a relationship between the horizontal length of the clamp and the size of the U bolt. This equation defines the length as equal to the radius of the U bolt arc, plus the bolt diameter, plus 0.5.

Solved under constrained sketch requiring 6 dimensions / constraints.

Your profile should look like the one shown in Figure 8-5 if you turned the dimensions display to **Equations**. The dimension numbering scheme in your profile depends upon the order you used to construct the model and may be different from the one shown in Figure 8-5. In the next step you will give the clamp a thickness of 0.25 units.

Select first item: *Pick point P2. You may need to zoom in closer to be able to accurately pick this line.*

Select second item or place dimension: *Pick a point to the right of the line at P2 in Figure 8-5.*

Undo/Hor/Ver/Align/Par/Dimension value <##.##>: **.25**↵ *Give the clamp a thickness of 0.25 units.*

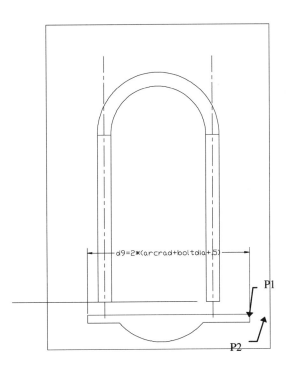

Figure 8-5 *Clamp profile with parametric dimensions*

Solved under constrained sketch requiring 5 dimensions / constraints.

Your profile should look like Figure 8-6.

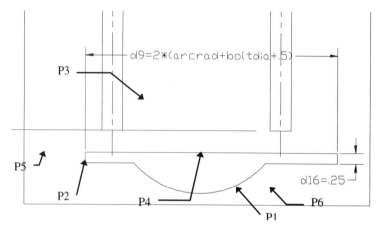

Figure 8-6 *Clamp profile*

Next, you will locate the centerpoint of the arc. You need to specify both the horizontal and vertical locations. For this part, the horizontal location of the centerpoint should be at the midpoint of the horizontal baseline. The vertical location should be on the horizontal base line.

Select first item: *Select P1 in Figure 8-6, any point on the arc.*

Select second item or place dimension: *Select P2. This will give you the horizontal distance of the arc's centerpoint from the left side of the part.*

Specify dimension placement: *Select P3, to place the dimension above the horizontal baseline.*

Undo/Hor/Ver/Align/Par/Dimension value <X.X>: **=d#/2,** *where # is the dimension number for the upper horizontal dimension. In Figure 8-6, the dimension number is 9, so you would enter =d9/2.*

Solved under constrained sketch requiring 4 dimensions / constraints.

Next, you will specify the vertical location of the arc's centerpoint.

Select first item: *Select P1 from Figure 8-6, any point on the arc.*

Select second item or place dimension: *Select P4. This will give you the vertical distance of the arc's centerpoint from the horizontal line.*

Specify dimension placement: *Select P5, to place the dimension on the left side of the drawing.*

Undo/Hor/Ver/Align/Par/Dimension value <X.X>: **0.↵** *This will locate the arc's centerpoint on the horizontal line.*

Solved under constrained sketch requiring 3 dimensions/ constraints.

The final dimension required to fully define the arc is the radius. For this part, you will specify the clamp radius as a function of the radius of the U bolt, **arcrad**. In order to allow room for drilling holes in the clamp, you will make the radius of the clamp equal to the U bolt radius minus .5 units.

Select first item: *Select P1 from Figure 8-6, any point on the arc.*

Select second item or place dimension: *Select P6. This will locate the radius dimension outside the arc.*

Undo/Dimension value <X.X>: **=arcrad-.5.**↵ *This will define the arc's radius as a function of the global variable,* **arcrad**.

```
Solved under constrained sketch requiring 2
dimensions/constraints.
```

Your sketch should look like the one in Figure 8-7. Notice that the clamp's arc (*d19* in Figure 8-7) has been assigned a radius as a function of the global parameter, **arcrad**.

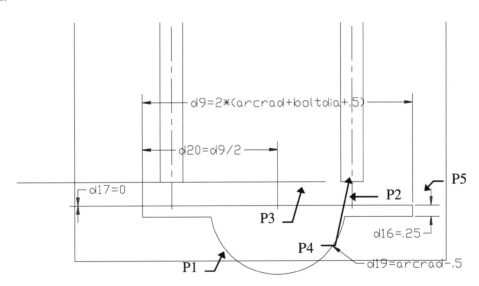

Figure 8-7 *Fully dimensioned clamp profile*

The basic geometry of the clamp is now fully defined. Yet, Designer reports that two more dimensions are needed to fully constrain the sketch. Since this clamp is not the initial profile in your model, you are required to locate the clamp with respect to the base part, the U-bolt. Therefore, you need to specify both the horizontal and vertical location of the clamp with respect to the U-bolt. The easiest way to specify this location is to reference the centerpoint of the arc with respect to the axes of the U bolt.

Select first item: *Select P1 in Figure 8-7, any point on the arc.*

Select second item or place dimension: *Select P2 to locate the horizontal distance of the arc's centerpoint from the work axis through the U bolt shaft.*

140 Assembly Modeling Using Parametric Relationships

Specify dimension placement: *Select P3 in Figure 8-7, to place the dimension on the left side of the work axis.*

Undo/Hor/Ver/Align/Par/Dimension value <X.X>: **=arcrad**↵ *(If Designer does not display a horizontal dimension, you will need to type* **H**↵ *before entering a dimension value.) Assigning a value equal to the global parameter,* **arcrad***, will locate the arc's centerpoint in the same horizontal location as the U bolt centerline (remember, the U bolt has a radius of* **arcrad***).*

Solved under constrained sketch requiring 1 dimensions/constraints.

The only remaining dimension you need to fully define the clamp profile is the vertical location of the clamp in relationship to the U bolt. For this model, you will locate the clamp .5 units below the U bolt.

Select first item: *Select P1, any point on the arc.*

Select second item or place dimension: *Select P4 in Figure 8-7. This will give you the vertical distance of the arc's centerpoint from the base of the U bolt.*

Specify dimension placement: *Select P5, to place the dimension on the right side of the drawing.*

Undo/Hor/Ver/Align/Par/Dimension value <X.X>: **.5**↵ *This will locate the arc's centerpoint .5 units below the base of the U bolt. Remember, if Designer does not give you a vertical dimension, you will need to type* **V**↵ *before entering the dimension value.*

Solved fully constrained sketch.

Your clamp profile is now completely defined and should look like Figure 8-8.

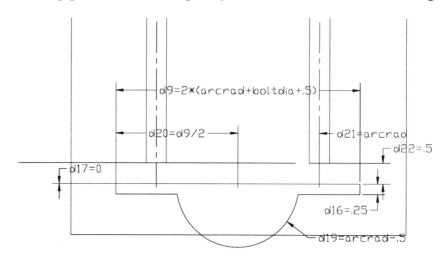

Figure 8-8 *Fully dimensioned/constrained profile of clamp piece*

Let's stop for a moment and look at the relationships between the global parameters and the geometry for the profile you just created. The radius of the clamp's arc is a function of the global parameter, **arcrad**, and can only be changed by changing the definition of this parameter. Since the U bolt geometry is also a function of **arcrad**, any changes in the value of **arcrad** will modify the geometry of *both* the clamp and the U bolt by the same amount. Therefore, global parameters and equations can be used to maintain geometric relationships in assembly models, even as you modify one part of the model's geometry.

Step Three: Extrude the Profile to Create a Solid Feature

Use **Designer>Features>Extrude** to turn the clamp profile into a solid feature. Instead of entering a numerical value into the dialog box for extrusion distance, use the global parameter **arcrad** as the distance to extrude. Since the profile was located on a work plane in line with the axes of the U bolt, you will need to specify a **Mid Plane** termination, rather the default **Blind** termination. **Mid Plane** will extrude the profile equal distances on either side of the sketch plane. Therefore, the total extrusion distance will be **2*arcrad** since Designer extrudes equal distances from the mid plane.

Complete the **Designer Extrusion** dialogue box to look like Figure 8-9 and select **OK** to extrude.

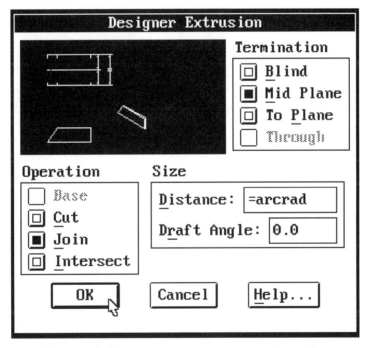

Figure 8-9 *Designer Extrusion dialogue box*

Use **Designer>Part Viewing>Iso** to display the feature in isometric view. Your part should look like the one shown in Figure 8-10.

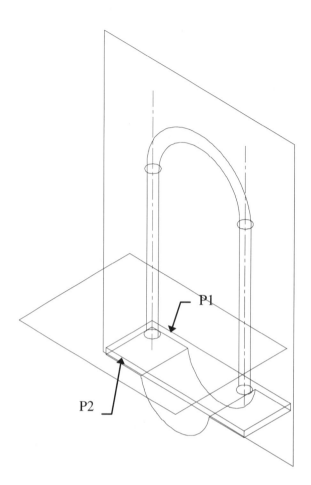

Figure 8-10 *Isometric view of extruded clamp profile*

Step Four: Modify the Clamp

You will use the Designer **adhole** command to "cut" a cylinder through the front face of the clamp. By specifying a hole diameter .25 units less than the diameter of the arc, you will create a clamp with a curved part of .25 units thickness.

Use **Designer>Features>Hole** from the pull-down menus, to create a hole through the front of the part. You will specify a hole placement concentric with the arc on the front of the part. Specify a diameter as a function of the global parameter, **arcrad**. Type in **=2*(arcrad-.5)-.25** for the value of the hole diameter.

The completed **Designer Hole** dialogue box should look like the one shown in Figure 8-11.

Introduction 143

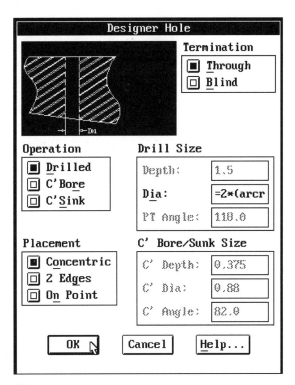

Figure 8-11 *Designer Hole dialogue box*

Step Five: Add Drilled Holes and Fillets

Two operations remain to finish the clamp assembly. You need to drill two holes that are in line with the U bolt and put a fillet on all four corners of the clamp.

Add Work Points to the Clamp

Work points will be placed on the clamp to help you locate the remaining two holes in line with the shafts of the U-bolt. Before placing these work points, you need to move the sketch plane to the top of the clamp.

Be sure that your current viewpoint is the isometric view of the part. Use the **Designer>Part Viewing>Isometric** to get a better view of the part.

Select **Designer>Sketch>Sketch Plane** from the pull-down menus.

Xy/Yz/Zx/Ucs/<Select work plane or planar face>: *Select a point P1, from Figure 8-10, on the top surface of the clamp.*

X/Y/Z/<Select work axis or straight edge>: *Select a point on the front edge of the part, P2, as shown in Figure 8-10.*

Rotate/<Accept>: *Accept the displayed orientation of the UCS or Rotate to see other orientations.*

The work points will be easier to locate if you change the view of your clamp to the new sketch plane. Use the **Designer>Part Viewing>Sketch** to change the viewpoint. The new view of the clamp should look like Figure 8-12.

144 Assembly Modeling Using Parametric Relationships

Use **Designer>Features>Work Point** to place a work points at the approximate locations shown in the figure below. Try to locate the work points near the centers of the U bolt shafts.

Location on sketch plane: *Place the work point as shown in Figure 8-12.*

The exact locations of the work points will be constrained when you add two parametric dimensions in the next step. These work points will be used as aids for locating the drilled holes in the clamp.

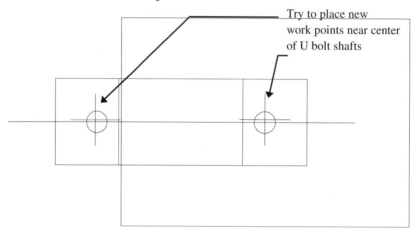

Figure 8-12 *View of clamp from current sketch plane showing new work points*

Locating each work point requires two dimensions and/or constraints. The work point locations are easier to specify if you switch back to the isometric view of the clamp using **Designer>Part Viewing>Isometric.** Your model should have the same orientation as Figure 8-13. You may find that the work points are easier to locate if you first turn off the display of the work planes.

Select **Designer>Display>Work Plane>Off** from the pull-down menus. *This will turn off the work plane display.*

If necessary use the AutoCAD **Zoom** command to enlarge the work points and circles. You will next use the **adpardim** command to give each work point the same X- and Y-coordinate as the centerpoint of each U bolt shaft.

Select **Designer>Sketch>Add Dimension** from the pull-down menus to add two dimensions to each work point.

Select first item: *Select a circle.*

Select second item or place dimension: *Select the "vertical" cross hair of the work point.*

Undo/Hor/Ver/Align/Par/Dimension value <##.##>: **0.↵** *Specify a value of 0 for the horizontal distance. If you are not prompted with a "horizontal" dimension, press* **H↵** *to toggle to a horizontal option.*

```
Solved under constrained sketch requiring 1
dimensions/constraints.
```

Select first item: *Select a circle.*

Select second item or place dimension: *Select the "horizontal" cross hair of the work point.*

Undo/Hor/Ver/Align/Par/Dimension value <##.##>: **0↵** *Specify a value of 0 for the vertical distance. If you are not prompted with a "vertical" dimension, press* **V↵** *to toggle to a vertical option.*

Solved fully constrained sketch.

Repeat this sequence of commands for the remaining work point axis. When finished, your model should look like Figure 8-13. The work points are now located in the same line as the centerline of the U bolt shafts.

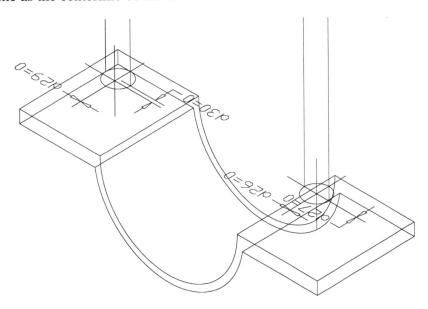

Figure 8-13 *Fully constrained work points on clamp surface*

Fillet the Corners of the Clamp

Creating fillets will be easier if you set up an isometric view of the part and use the AutoCAD **zoom** command to enlarge the corners you are trying to fillet. Use the Designer **adfillet** command to fillet the sharp corners of the clamp.

Select **Designer>Features>Fillet** from the Designer pull-down menus.

Select an edge: *Select one of the four corners of the clamp.*

Select an edge: *Select a second corner of the clamp.*

Select an edge: *Select a third corner of the clamp.*

Select an edge: *Select the remaining corner of the clamp.*

146 Assembly Modeling Using Parametric Relationships

Select an edge: ↵ *will complete the selection.*

Fillet radius <current>: **0.5**↵ *This will fillet each corner with a radius equal to 0.5 units.*

When finished, your model should look like Figure 8-14.

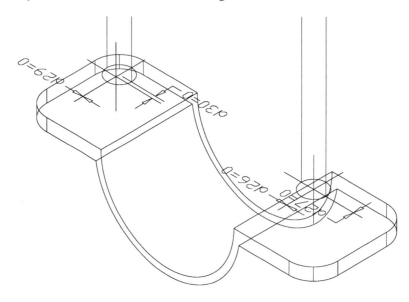

Figure 8-14 *Detail view of clamp*

Drill the Holes

The final step in creating the clamp assembly is to drill the holes through the work points you previously defined. Because the clamp and shaft must have a "clearance fit," you will define the clamp holes to be slightly larger than the shaft diameter. Because you are using parametric modeling, global parameters can be used for these diameter dimensions. Global parameters will be used to specify the dimensions of the holes as a function of **boltdia**. Therefore, if you modify the model by changing the diameter of the bolt shaft, the hole diameter will automatically be changed to maintain the same clearance.

Create a new global parameter

Prior to using any global parameter, you first have to define the parameter using the **adparam** command. You will use a new parameter, called **clearance**, which specifies the clearance between the bolt hole and the bolt shaft diameter.

To execute this command type **adparam**↵ at the **Command:** prompt, or use the Designer pull-down menus:

Select **Designer>Parameters>Create** from the pull-down menus.

Enter equation: **clearance=.1**↵ *This will create a new global parameter named "clearance" and assign a value of 0.1 to this parameter. Therefore, the hole diameter will always be larger than the shaft diameter.*

Designer will respond with:

`Parameter clearance created: current value = =.1`

Enter equation: ↵ *This will return you to the* **adpardim** *prompt:*

To view the current global parameters being used in your model, you will list the parameters.

Create/Delete/List/Import/Export/<eXit>: **L**↵ *Type L to list the parameters you just created. Designer will show all the parameters in a table format.*

	Parameter Name	Definitions
1)	boltlen	=6
2)	arcrad	=2
3)	boltdia	=.5
4)	clearance	=.1

Create/Delete/List/Import/Export/<eXit>: **L**↵ *Type X to exit.*

The Designer **adhole** command will be used to drill the holes through the clamp.

Use **Designer>Features>Holes** to create a **Through** hole with the **On Point** operation. For the hole diameter, specify a value of **=boltdia +clearance**. This option locates the hole on the work point that you previously defined.

Complete the **Designer Hole** dialogue box so it looks like the one shown in Figure 8-15.

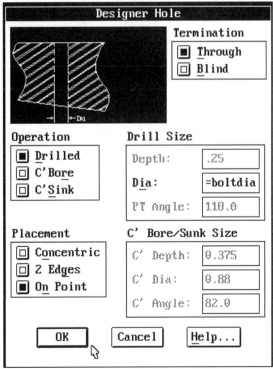

Figure 8-15 *Designer Hole dialogue box using global parametric equations to define diameter*

Repeat this operation for both holes. The finished clamp should look similar to Figure 8-16.

To put the finishing touches on your model, you can now use Designer's automatic drafting features, covered previously, to create a layout of the clamp assembly with orthographic and isometric views. This layout should look like Figure 8-17.

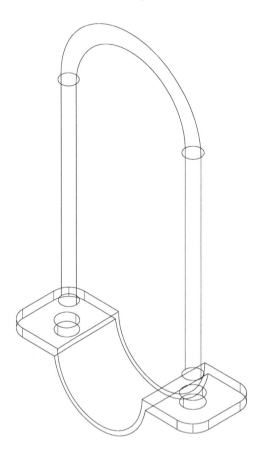

Figure 8-16 *Completed clamp/U bolt assembly*

End of Chapter Summary

You have defined global parameters that were used in parametric equations to link the geometry of a clamp to that of a U bolt created in the previous lesson. By using parameters, rather than numeric values, a design engineer has much greater control over the modification and editing of the model.

The advantage of this method over conventional construction techniques is that if you now need to modify the part, you simply change the value of the global parameters and all corresponding geometry is changed based upon the mathematical relationships used to define the dimensions.

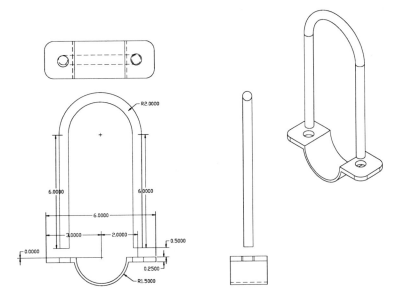

Figure 8-17 *Complete engineering drawing of clamp/U bolt assembly*

Exercises

Use parametric relationships to create the following Designer assembly models. Define the geometry of mating parts parametrically, so the parts will always fit together.

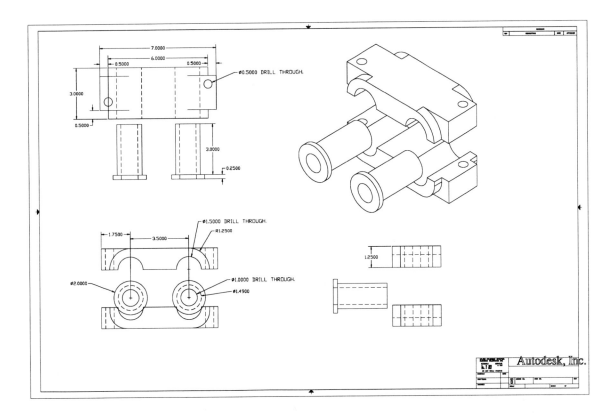

150 Assembly Modeling Using Parametric Relationships

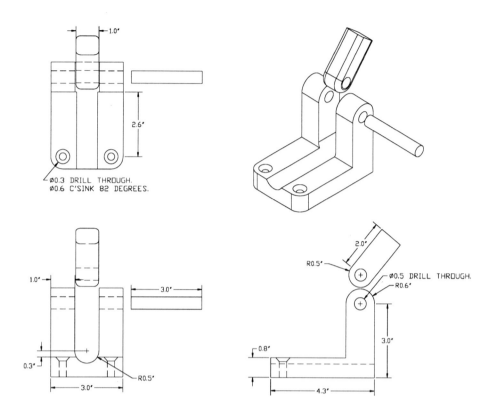
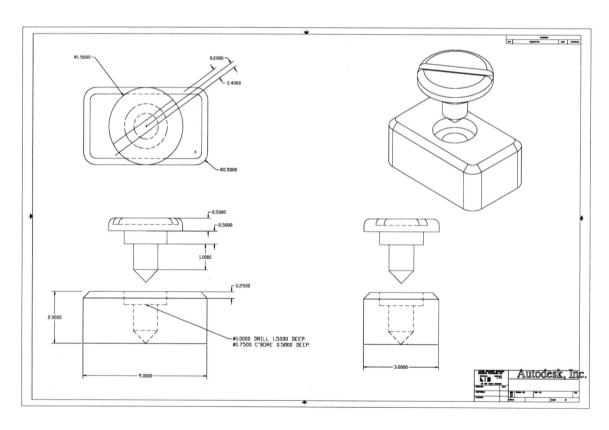

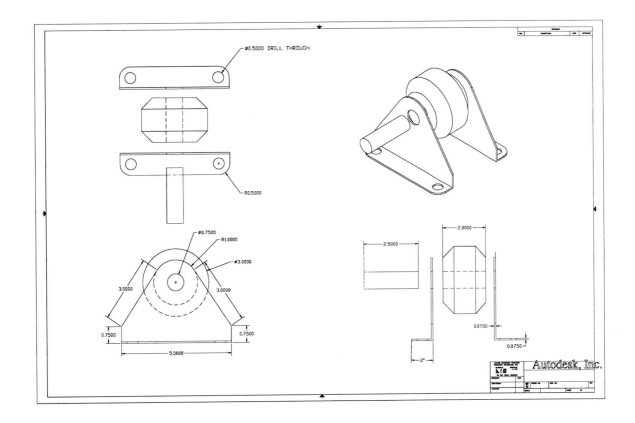

Appendix

Commands

This chapter describes the AutoCAD Designer commands.

ADACTPART

ADACTPART lets you switch between parts in a multiple part drawing. This command is only valid in Part mode.

Command: **adactpart**
Select part: *Select the part to make active.*

To show the currently active part, use ADSHOWACT.

ADADDCON

ADADDCON lets you add parametric constraints to paths and profiles for features. ADADDCON works only on the active profile. Constraints, however, are permanent even after the sketch set is no longer active. Use ADDELCON to remove constraints.

Command: **adaddcon**
Hor/Ver/PErp/PAr/Tan/CL/CN/PRoj/Join/XValue/YValue/Radius/<exit>:
  Enter an option.

When you create a profile or path, AutoCAD Designer numbers each entity in the sketch. ADSHOWCON displays these numbers, as well as symbols for the constraints applied to the entity. If a constraint is between two entities, the number of the partner entity follows the constraint symbol. In figure 5–1, the N3 constraint shows entity 6 has a center point coincident with entity 3.

Commands

Figure 5-1. Constraint symbol

AutoCAD Designer allows the following constraints.

Hor   Horizontal lines are parallel to the *X* axis. (H symbol.) This option prompts you to select the line to which you want the constraint applied.

Ver   Vertical lines are parallel to the *Y* axis. (V symbol.) This option prompts you to select the line to which you want the constraint applied.

PErp   Perpendicular lines have slopes 90 degrees from each other. (L symbol.) Select the line to which you want another line to be perpendicular, and then select the line to be perpendicular.

PAr   Parallel lines have the same slope and orientation. (P symbol.) Select the two lines you want parallel.

Tan   The slope of two entities is identical at the point where they meet. Allowable pairs are two arcs or circles or one line and one arc or circle. (T symbol.) This option prompts you to select the entities to which you want the constraint applied.

CL   Collinear entities fall on the same line. (C symbol.) Select the two lines you want colinear.

CN   Concentric arcs and circles have coincident center points. (N symbol.) Select the two arcs or circles to which you want the constraint applied.

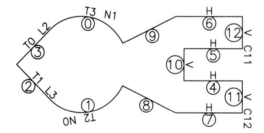

Figure 5-2. Examples of constraint symbols

ADADDCON

Chapter 5

PRoj The selected point of an entity joins the unbounded definition of a second entity. (J symbol.) Select the endpoint of a line or arc to project, and then select the line to project it to. To select an arc or circle centerpoint instead of an endpoint, use the **Center** mode of the AutoCAD OSNAP command before you select the arc or circle. Then select the line to project it to.

In the following example, to create the V-shaped notch in the top center of the fixture, you can use the project constraint to project the point on the V to the work plane running through the fixture.

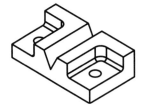 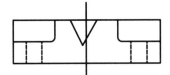 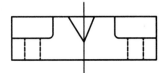

Figure 5–3.

Join The selected end points are coincident. Use this option to close a gap between geometry in your sketch set. (A joined constraint does not show a symbol.) Select the endpoint of one line or arc to join and another arc or line endpoint.

XValue The center points of circles have the same X coordinate. (X symbol.) Select two circles to which you want the option applied.

YValue The center points of circles have the same Y coordinate. (Y symbol.) Select two circles to which you want the option applied.

Radius Arcs and circles have the same radius. You can apply this constraint only after you have dimensioned one or more radii for arcs or circles. (R symbol.) Select the arcs and circles you want to have equal radii.

The constraint options for ADADDCON are identical to those used by ADPROFILE and ADPATH.

Commands

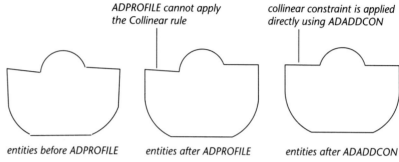

Figure 5–4. Using ADADDCON after ADPROFILE

Use ADADDCON in the following situations:

- To add constraints between existing model edges, work planes, or work axes that are not part of the selected sketch geometry
- To clean up loosely sketched geometry where AutoCAD Designer doesn't make the assumptions you expect

See chapter 1, "Fundamentals," for more information on using constraints.

ADANNOTE

ADANNOTE lets you create, delete, and move annotations on an AutoCAD Designer drawing and add or remove items belonging to the annotation. Annotation includes callout bubbles, centerlines, and surface finish symbols. Create the text and geometry for the annotation with AutoCAD and use ADANNOTE to attach it parametrically to drawing views.

This parametric location automatically updates so that the annotation is not obscured when geometry moves on the drawing page. Annotations also move with the drawing view when you use ADMOVEVIEW.

Command: **adannote**
Create/Delete/Move/Add/Remove: *Enter an option.*

Chapter 5

Create   Establishes a single annotation entity from selected AutoCAD entities such as text, lines, circles, and blocks and attaches the annotation to a part edge in a drawing view. Create and position the AutoCAD entities before attaching them to the AutoCAD Designer drawing view.

Select entities to make an annotation.

Select objects: *Select 2D AutoCAD entities that you want to make into an annotation item. Press ⏎ to end selection.*

Locate point to attach annotation. *Pick a point on the part geometry within the view.*

Leader start point: *Pick any point to start the leader.*

Leader end point: *Pick any point to end the leader.*

Next leader vertex: *Continue entering vertices and press ⏎ to stop.*

The leader start point and the attachment point are not necessarily the same point on the drawing. The attachment point must be a vertex on the part geometry, an endpoint or a center point, but the leader start point can be placed anywhere. In the example below, the leader points to a surface on the part, but the attachment point is the center of the edge as indicated.

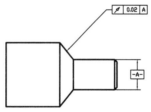

Figure 5–5.

Attachment points cannot be made to silhouette edges on the part.

Delete   Removes annotations and related AutoCAD entities from the AutoCAD database.

Select annotation by selecting any of its entities: *Pick an annotation item. The annotation is deleted.*

ADANNOTE

A-5

Commands

Move — Moves the selected annotation around the drawing, maintaining its attachment to the drawing view or part edge.

Select annotation by selecting any of its entities: *Pick an annotation item.*

Note location: *Pick a new location for the annotation. This moves the annotation and the leader while keeping the start point fixed.*

Add — Adds the selected AutoCAD objects, such as text, lines, circles, and blocks to an existing annotation. Position the AutoCAD entities to be added to the annotation before using the Add option.

Select annotation by selecting any of its entities: *Pick an annotation item.*

Select entities to add to annotation.

Select objects: *Select any new 2D AutoCAD geometry or text to add to the annotation item. Press ⏎ to end object selection.*

Remove — Removes AutoCAD entities from an annotation entity without deleting the annotation.

Select items to remove from annotation.

Select objects: *Select any 2D AutoCAD geometry or text to delete from the annotation item. Press ⏎ to end object selection.*

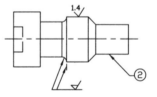

Figure 5–6. Annotation examples

ADASFCONV

ADASFCONV converts AutoCAD Designer parts into a collection of AutoSurf surfaces. The AutoSurf surfaces created inherit their properties from the AutoCAD Designer part they are created from. You can also use ADASFCONV to delete the selected AutoCAD Designer parts

Chapter 5

after creating the AutoSurf surfaces. You can use this command with or without AutoSurf loaded.

Command: **adasfconv**

Select parts to convert.

Select objects: *Select the part(s)*.

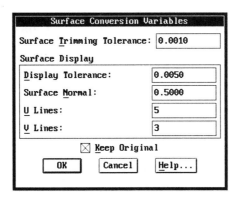

Figure 5–7. Surface Conversion Variables dialogue box

Surface Trimming Tolerance This tolerance is the value used when ADASFCONV chords NURBS curves from the AutoCAD Designer part into polylines. These polylines are used as borders to trim the AutoSurf surfaces. This value defaults to the current value of the AutoSurf system variable ASSYSTOL when AutoSurf is loaded. The default is 0.001 when AutoSurf is not loaded.

Surface Display Lets you set display options for the AutoSurf surfaces created. Values for these options are the defaults from the AutoSurf system variables when AutoSurf is loaded.

    Display Tolerance Sets the tolerance used for display lines for AutoSurf surfaces created by ADASFCONV. The default value is the current value of the AutoSurf system variable ASSURFDISP when AutoSurf is loaded, or 0.005 when AutoSurf is not loaded.

    Surface Normal Determines the length of the normal vector shown as part of the AutoSurf surface display. The default is the current setting of the AutoSurf system variable ASSURFVECTOR when AutoSurf is loaded, or 0.5 when it is not.

Commands

	U Lines	Sets the number of lines shown in the U direction of the AutoSurf surfaces created by ADASFCONV. The default is the current setting of the AutoSurf system variable ASSURFU when AutoSurf is loaded, or 5 when it is not.
	V Lines	Sets the number of lines shown in the V direction of the AutoSurf surfaces created by ADASFCONV. The default is the current setting of the AutoSurf system variable ASSURFV when AutoSurf is loaded, or 3 when it is not.
Keep original		Specifies whether ADASFCONV deletes the input AutoCAD Designer parts after creating the AutoSurf surfaces. The default setting is always checked. Input AutoCAD Designer parts are not deleted. To delete parts, select the checkbox so that is it not checked.

ADAXISDSP

ADAXISDSP is a toggle that displays all work axes of the active part. The axes are visible if ADAXISDSP is on. This command is only valid in part mode.

Command: **adaxisdsp**
OFf/<On>: *Enter an option.*

ADCHAMFER

ADCHAMFER creates a chamfer on the selected edge(s) of the active part.

Chapter 5

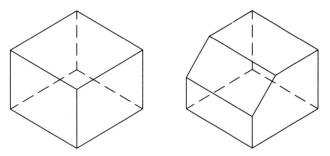

Figure 5–8. Active part before and after using ADCHAMFER

Command: **adchamfer**

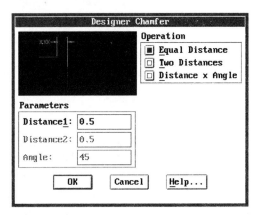

Figure 5–9. Designer Chamfer dialogue box

If the selection ends at a point where the end points of two entities join and are tangent continuous, AutoCAD Designer automatically extends the chamfer until it reaches a noncontinuous end.

Note: All chamfers created within a single pass of this command are a single feature controlled by one chamfer definition. ADDELFEAT removes all of them.

Commands

Operation		Determines the method for creating the chamfer.
	Equal Distance	Creates a chamfer at an equal distance along two surfaces meeting at the selected edge. Uses the Distance1 value in the Parameters area of the dialogue box.
		Select edge: *Select the edge to chamfer.*
		Select edge: *Continue selecting edges or press ⏎ to end selection.*
	Two Distances	Creates a chamfer designated by Distance1 and Distance2 values in the Parameters area of the dialogue box.
		Select edge: *Select the edge to chamfer.*
		Apply distance1 to highlighted face. *Select the face to which you want distance 1 applied.*
		Flip/<Accept>: *Select an option. Use the Flip option to switch the highlighted face.*
	Distance x Angle	Creates a chamfer defined by the Distance1 and Angle values in the Parameters area of the dialogue box.
		Select edge: *Select the edge to chamfer.*
		Apply distance value to highlighted face. *Select the face to which you want distance 1 applied.*
		Flip/<Accept>: *Select an option. Use the Flip option to switch the highlighted face.*
Parameters		Sets the values AutoCAD Designer uses to create the chamfer.
	Distance1	Enter the first distance for the chamfer.
	Distance2	Enter the second distance for the chamfer.
	Angle	Enter the angle for the chamfer.

ADCHAMFER

Chapter 5

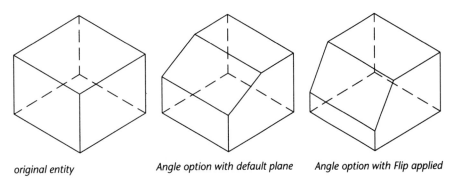

original entity   Angle option with default plane   Angle option with Flip applied

Figure 5–10. Flip/Accept options

ADDELCON

ADDELCON deletes constraints from the active sketch. Use this command to remove constraints and change the geometric relationships between sketched entities.

Command: **addelcon**
All/Select item to edit: *Enter an option.*

All	Removes all constraints from all entities in the active sketch.
Select item to edit	Displays the constraints for the selected entity. Select the constraint symbol you want to remove and press ⏎ to exit the command.

Note: Select constraints by picking directly on the constraint label.

ADDELFEAT

ADDELFEAT deletes features from the active part.

Command: **addelfeat**
Select feature to delete: *Select a feature.*

To select part geometry, pick an edge or non-hidden face belonging to the feature. To select a work plane, work point, or work axis, pick the displayed feature.

Commands

If the selected feature has dependent features, they will be deleted as well, unless you respond to the message by choosing not to continue.

ADDELFEAT works only on features on the active part, but doesn't delete the active part itself. Use the AutoCAD ERASE command to delete AutoCAD Designer parts.

Pick Toggling

AutoCAD Designer has picking methods that supplement AutoCAD picking. This is because AutoCAD Designer parts get complicated quickly and picking may be difficult. AutoCAD Designer picking methods are employed when you select features or faces on AutoCAD Designer parts in Part mode. For example, when you use ADDELFEAT and are prompted to pick a feature, AutoCAD Designer feature picking is employed.

These picking methods use toggling, which means that from a single pick, many possibilities are identified. AutoCAD Designer lets you toggle through all of these possibilities one by one until you get to the entity you want. Every time you pick a feature in AutoCAD Designer, the best choice is highlighted first and AutoCAD Designer prompts: Next/<Accept>. If you enter **n**, AutoCAD Designer highlights the next choice. However, the goal of AutoCAD Designer picking is to get the right choice on the very first pick.

Hints for Successful Feature Picking:

1. Pick right in the middle of the feature, keeping the pickbox away from any edges. Even if the feature is on the back of the part you are likely to get it as the first choice.

2. If the feature is near the back of the part and there are a lot of features between it and you, pick on one of the feature's edges. Always try to get an edge that belongs to that feature alone.

ADDELREF

ADDELREF deletes reference dimensions from drawing views. It has no effect on parametric dimensions.

Command: **addelref**
Select view dimension: *Select the reference dimension to delete.*

Chapter 5

ADDELVIEW

ADDELVIEW deletes the specified drawing view and all of its dependent views. You must be in Drawing mode to use this command. (See "ADMODE" on page 303.)

Command: **addelview**
Select view to delete: *Select a view.*

If the selected drawing view has dependent views, you can delete the view and its dependent views, or only the selected view.

ADDIMATT

ADDIMATT lets you modify the appearance, precision, and tolerance of drawing view dimensions.

Command: **addimatt**
Select dimension to edit: *Select a dimension.*

Figure 5-11. Designer Dimension Options dialogue box

Commands

Style	Select type of units from the pop-up list.
Scientific	1.55E+01
Decimal	15.50 (to the number of decimal places set by the precision)
Engineering	1'-3.50"
Architectural	1'-3 1/2"
Fractional	15 1/2
Precision	Controls the number of decimal places.
Text Height	Sets the height of the dimension text.
Prefix	Specifies the dimension prefix.
Suffix	Specifies the dimension suffix.
Layer	Displays a layers list from which you select the layer for the dimensions.

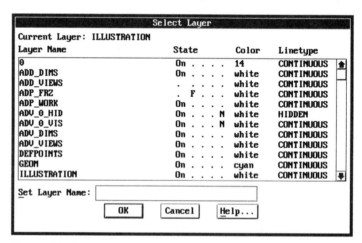

Figure 5-12. Select Layer dialogue box

Tolerances Displays the Dimension Tolerances dialogue box that lets you set the type and variable.

Chapter 5

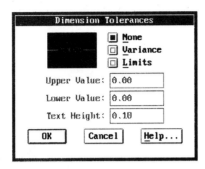

Figure 5–13. Dimension Tolerances dialogue box

Text Placement Controls arrow and text placement.

Figure 5–14. Text Placement dialogue box

Extension Line Controls extension line suppression. Indicate the sup-
Suppression pression you want to use.

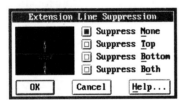

Figure 5–15. Extension Line Suppression dialogue box

Flip Direction Flips the location of the dimension and text.

Save as Default Sets the attributes for future dimensions.

ADDIMATT A-15

ADDIMDSP

ADDIMDSP changes the display mode for dimensions of all parts and sketches without affecting the drawing so that you can see the dimension parameters to use in equations for other dimensions.

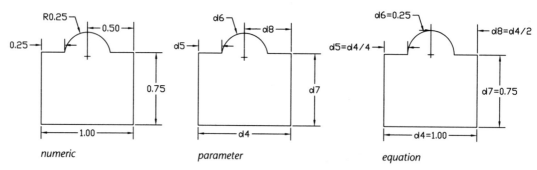

Figure 5-16. Displaying dimensions

Command: **addimdsp**
Parameters/Equations/<Numeric>: *Enter an option.*

Parameters Shows only the dimension parameter name.

Equations Shows the equation for dimensions governed by an equation.

Numeric Shows only the current numeric value.

ADEDITFEAT

ADEDITFEAT displays and modifies the dimension values of the active part's features. You can use equations for dimension values in the same manner as for ADMODDIM (see page 302). ADEDITFEAT only works in Part mode.

Command: **adeditfeat**
Sketch/<Select feature>: *Select the feature to edit or enter* **s**.
Select dimension to change: *Select the dimension.*

Chapter 5

Sketch   Lets you select the feature whose sketch you want to edit. AutoCAD Designer rolls back the part to the feature's sketch and resets the sketch plane. You can edit dimensions and constraints but you cannot make changes to the geometry.

Select feature: *Select the feature.*

For more information regarding editing feature sketches, refer to "Modifying Features" in Chapter 1, "Fundamentals."

Note: You must execute the ADUPDATE command to regenerate the part to the new values. You can edit as many dimension values and features as you want before updating with ADUPDATE.

The Designer Hole dialogue box opens when the feature you select is a Hole feature.

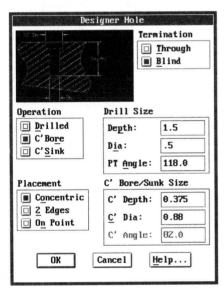

Figure 5–17. Designer Hole dialogue box

Pick Toggling

AutoCAD Designer has picking methods that supplement AutoCAD picking. This is because AutoCAD Designer parts get complicated quickly and picking may be difficult. AutoCAD Designer picking methods are employed when you select features or faces on AutoCAD Designer parts in Part mode. For example, when you choose ADEDIT-FEAT and are prompted to pick a feature, AutoCAD Designer feature picking is employed.

Commands

These picking methods use toggling, which means that from a single pick, many possibilities are identified. AutoCAD Designer lets you toggle through all of these possibilities one by one until you get to the entity you want. Every time you pick a feature in AutoCAD Designer, the best choice will highlight first and AutoCAD Designer will prompt: Next/<Accept>. If you enter **n**, AutoCAD Designer will highlight the next choice. However, the goal of AutoCAD Designer picking is to get the right choice on the very first pick.

Hints for Successful Feature Picking:

1. Pick right in the middle of the feature, keeping the pickbox away from any edges. Even if the feature is on the back of the part you are likely to get it as the first choice.

2. If the feature is near the back of the part and there are a lot of features between it and you, pick on one of the feature's edges. Always try to get an edge that belongs to that feature alone.

ADEDITVIEW

ADEDITVIEW modifies the scale, associated text, and hidden line display of the selected drawing view. You can also use ADEDITVIEW to resize the boundaries of a detail view. You must be in Drawing mode to use this command. (See ADMODE on page 303.)

Command: **adeditview**

Select view: *Select a view.*

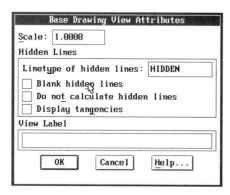

Figure 5–18. Base Drawing View Attributes dialogue box

This dialogue box is context sensitive. The following description lists all options. The dialogue box you see might not display every option.

A-18 ADEDITVIEW

Chapter 5

Scale — Lets you change the drawing view scale.

Hidden Lines — Lets you change the line type to hidden lines, blank hidden lines, or suppresses calculations of hidden lines.

Display Tangencies — Lets you change the display of tangent *edges* in the view. See figure 5-19.

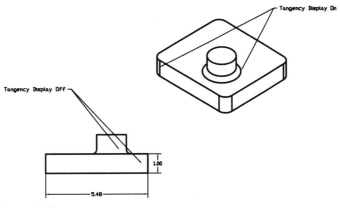

Figure 5-19.

View Label — Lets you edit the view label.

Resize — Lets you resize the detail view boundaries.

ADEXTRUDE

ADEXTRUDE creates an extruded solid feature from the active sketch.

Command: **adextrude**

 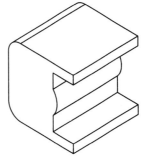

Figure 5-20. Extruded profile

Commands

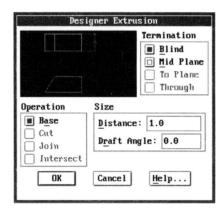

Figure 5–21. Designer Extrusion dialogue box

Termination	Determines the method for ending the extrusion.	
	Blind	Extrudes the feature to a specified depth.
	Mid Plane	Extrudes the profile equally in both directions, terminating at the specified overall depth.
	To Plane	Defines the extrusion to the specified planar face or work plane.
	Through	Cuts all the way through the solid part. This option is available for extruded cuts and intersects only.
Operation	Specifies the Boolean method for creating the extrusion.	
	Base	Adds material, creating the first feature of a part.
	Cut	Removes material from the active part.
	Join	Adds material to the active part. Select the type of join.
	Intersect	Creates a new feature from the shared volume of the existing part and the Extrude feature.
Size	Specifies the value for the extrusion.	
	Distance	Enter the distance for the extrusion.
	Draft Angle	Enter the draft angle. A negative number creates a negative draft.

Chapter 5

Before you create an extruded feature, you must create an active sketch profile with ADPROFILE. Sketches must be single, closed boundaries, using any combination of new sketch geometry, existing model edges, work planes, or work axes. Your profile cannot contain internal islands.

AutoCAD Designer uses AutoCAD layers to control the display of sketch geometry and dimensions. Whenever a sketch is turned into a feature with ADREVOLVE, ADEXTRUDE, or ADSWEEP, AutoCAD Designer places the solid part and new feature on the current layer. AutoCAD Designer hides the sketch geometry and dimensions for the feature on the ADP_FRZ layer so they can be redisplayed by ADEDITFEAT.

Warning: Don't edit the contents of this layer. Doing so can permanently destroy or corrupt the modeling information in your drawing.

ADFILLET

ADFILLET creates a rolling ball fillet on the selected edge(s) of the active part. A single radius controls the fillet.

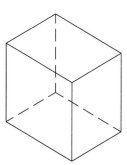 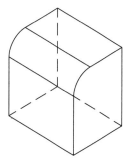

Figure 5–22. Active part before and after using ADFILLET

Command: **adfillet**
Select an edge: *Select the edge you want to fillet.*
Select an edge: *Select another edge you want to fillet or press ⏎ to complete the selection.*
Fillet radius <current>: *Enter the radius for the fillet(s).*

Commands

ADFILLET places both rounds and fillets on the selected edges. Select as many edges as you want for each execution of ADFILLET. If the selected edge ends at a point where the end points of two entities join and are tangent continuous, AutoCAD Designer automatically extends the fillet until it reaches a noncontinuous end.

ADFIXPT

ADFIXPT fixes a point on the active sketch so it is immovable in *XYZ* space relative to all other sketch entities. The fixed point of the sketch in a part's base feature becomes the 3D anchor for the part in the World Coordinate System (WCS).

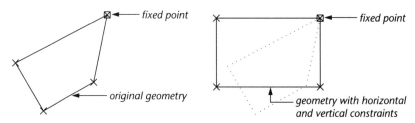

Figure 5–23. Geometry movement around the fixed point

Command: **adfixpt**

Specify new fixed point for active sketch: *Select the point you want fixed.*

Object snap modes should not be used with the ADFIXPT command. AutoCAD Designer will automatically pick the end point of a line or the center point of an arc or circle.

When you change a sketch by adding or changing constraints and dimensions, the geometry moves to match the change. One point remains fixed, and the geometry moves around it. Unless you select the fixed point yourself, ADFIXPT, ADPROFILE, and ADPATH will choose a point automatically.

Once the point is fixed, use AutoCAD commands to move the entire sketch and the fixed point.

ADFRZDIM

ADFRZDIM hides the specified dimension on a drawing. The dimension remains frozen even if the drawing is updated.

Command: **adfrzdim**
Freeze dimensions All /View/<Select>: *Enter an option.*

All Selects all dimensions.

View Selects a view.

Select Selects a dimension to freeze.

All dimensions used for a solid part appear in drawing views. You can't erase them because they control the parametric design. You can use ADFRZDIM if you want to hide some dimensions.

You can use ADREFDIM to create additional drawing dimensions while in Drawing mode. Use a combination of parametric dimensions and reference dimensions to completely dimension a part to standard.

To redisplay the frozen dimensions, use ADTHAWDIM.

ADHOLE

ADHOLE creates a drilled, counterbored, or countersunk hole in the active part.

 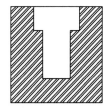 

drilled   counterbore   countersink

Figure 5–24. Hole types

Command: **adhole**

Commands

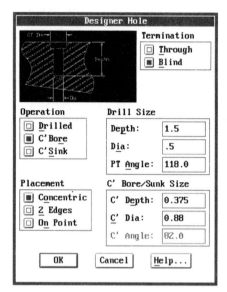

Figure 5–25. Designer Hole dialogue box

Termination	Determines the method for ending the hole.	
	Through	Creates a hole from the selected planar surface through the entire part.
	Blind	Creates a hole of the specified depth, beginning at the selected planar surface or work plane.
Operation	Determines the type of hole.	
	Drilled	Creates a hole with the specified diameter.
	C'Bore	Creates a hole of the specified diameter, counterbore depth, and counterbore diameter.
	C'Sink	Creates a hole of the specified diameter, countersink diameter, and countersink angle.
Drill Size	Enter the values for the depth, diameter, and point angle in the entry boxes in this section.	

A-24   ADHOLE

Chapter 5

Placement		Determines how AutoCAD Designer places the holes.
	Concentric	Locates the hole on a work plane or planar face perpendicular to the axis of the selected curved face. The selected curved face must be a cylinder, cone, or torus.

                                          X/Y/Z/Ucs/Select work plane or planar face:
                                          Select concentric edge:

	2 Edges	Places the hole at a user-defined distance from two edges bounding a common face.

                                          Select first edge:
                                          Select second edge:
                                          Select hole location:
                                          Distance from first edge <3.1347>:
                                          Distance from second edge <1.567>:

	On Point	Places the hole on the selected work point with its axis perpendicular to the sketch plane of the work point.

                                          Select work point:
                                          Direction Flip/<Accept>

C'Bore/Sunk SIze	When you have specified counter bored or countersunk holes, enter the values for the depth, diameter, and angle in the entry boxes in this section.

ADHOLE does not require an active sketch plane like ADEXTRUDE, ADREVOLVE, and ADSWEEP. AutoCAD Designer automatically creates the sketch plane when you select the work plane, planar face, or work point on the active part.

ADHOLENOTE

ADHOLENOTE creates a standard note with diametral depth and angle information for the selected hole in the drawing.

Command: **adholenote**
Select arc or circle of hole feature: *Do so.*
Location for hole note: *Pick a location.*

The dimension values for the Hole feature appear in a note with a leader. You can't change the hole size in Drawing mode. Instead, return to Part mode (see ADMODE on page 303) and edit the Hole feature with ADEDITFEAT. Then the subsequent AutoCAD Designer ADUPDATE updates the note.

ADISOLINES

ADISOLINES controls the display of the wire representation of a part, which uses isolines to help you visualize the curved faces. ADISOLINES controls two variables: ADISOCYL and ADISONURB.

When you want to update the isoline display, turn ADMESH off and select the part.

Command: **adisolines**
Isolines for cones, cylinders, and tori <2>: *Enter the number of isolines to display on these surface types.*
Isolines for nurbs <0>: *Enter the number of isolines to display on a NURBS surface.*

Note: Even though isolines are not true edges, you can select a part face by picking one of its isolines.

ADLIST

ADLIST provides information on parts, features, and drawing views.

Command: **adlist**
Feature/Part/<View>: *Select an option.*

Chapter 5

Feature	Allows you to list information on parental dependencies, children information, and a general listing of feature information. You must be in Part mode.

Select features: *Do so.*
Children/Parents/<List>: *Enter an option.*

Children	All features dependent on another feature for their existence.
Parents	Any feature that has children features.
<List>	A list of feature attributes.
Part	Lists the part ID(s) and feature information for the part you specify. You must be in Part mode.

ALl/Select/<ACtive>: *Enter an option.*

ALl	Every part in the current AutoCAD drawing (*.dwg* file).
Select	Any part you select.
<ACtive>	The active part.
View	List the type of drawing view, ID, view directions, centerpoint of the view, name of the visible layer, the names of hidden layers, the number of dependents, dimensions and notes, and how many parts are represented in the view. You must be in Drawing mode.

ADMAKEBASE

ADMAKEBASE converts the active AutoCAD Designer part into a static part and compresses the part information to take up less disk space.

Command: **admakebase**

Create base from highlighted part No/<Yes>: *Select an option.*

When a part becomes static, you can't edit it with the dimensions used to create it. You can construct additional features on static parts as you can with standard AutoCAD Designer parts.

Because ADMAKEBASE does not allow you to edit part dimensions, you can use it to create catalog, standard, and stock parts that are commonly used as is.

ADMASSPROP

ADMASSPROP lists the mass properties for the specified part(s). This command is context sensitive. If you select a single part, an interactive dialogue box appears where you can change the density to update the mass properties.

Command: **admassprop**

All/Select/<ACtive>: *Enter an option.*

If you specify a single part, a dialogue box similar to the following one appears:

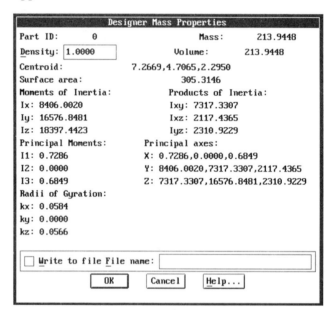

Figure 5–26. Mass properties dialogue box for a single part

If you select the Write to File button and enter a filename in the edit box, AutoCAD Designer writes the mass property information to the specified file.

Chapter 5

If you specify multiple parts, a dialogue box similar to the following one appears:

Figure 5–27. Mass properties dialogue box for multiple parts

For either dialogue box, you can change the density by entering a new value in the Density edit box.

The values in the dialogue box are not displayed with units. However, except for the centroid and the principal axes, they are not unitless. You determine the units for these calculations by the units you used when modeling the part and the units for the density. To keep the calculations meaningful, you should use the same length units in the density as you used during part modeling. For example, if you modeled the part in inches, enter the density in mass per unit inch.

ADMESH

The ON option of ADMESH displays the selected part in AutoCAD mesh representation within the specified tolerance—the maximum distance between the true part surface and the generated mesh elements. The OFf option (default) changes the solid part display from an AutoCAD mesh representation to a wireframe representation.

Commands

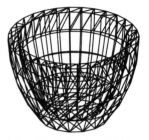

allowable deviation = 1   allowable deviation = 0.001

Figure 5–28. Mesh surfaces and deviation between facets and model

Command: **admesh**
OFf/ON: *Enter an option.*
Select parts to mesh: *Select a part.*

If you specify the ON option the following prompt appears:

Allowable deviation between facets and model <0.1>: *Enter a tolerance for the mesh.*

The AutoCAD mesh elements created with ADMESH can be used by other AutoCAD commands and other software packages to further process the AutoCAD Designer part. The AutoCAD RENDER, SHADE, and HIDE commands work on a meshed AutoCAD Designer model exactly as they do in AutoCAD.

Many third party rendering, manufacturing, and engineering analysis software accept the AutoCAD mesh representation.

ADMODDIM

ADMODDIM lets you modify dimension values on the active sketch or on the drawing. This command works only in parametric dimensions (those created in Part mode).

Command: **admoddim**
Select dimension to change: *Select the dimension you want to modify.*
New value for dimension <current>: *Enter the new value or equation.*
Select dimension to change: *Press ⏎ to finish modifying dimensions or select the next dimension you want to modify.*

To update the drawing and model after using ADMODDIM, you must use ADUPDATE. The update is automatic when working with an active sketch.

Chapter 5

To modify the dimensions of part features, use ADEDITFEAT.

Use ADMODDIM to set parametric dimensions equal to numerical values and equations. An equation can use any dimension parameter on the part to set up relationships between dimensions. Equations can also include global parameters.

AutoCAD Designer automatically defines a parameter for every dimension you create. ADDIMDSP lets you display dimension parameters while in Part mode.

ADMODE

ADMODE controls whether Part or Drawing mode is in effect.

Command: **admode**
Part/<Drawing>: *Enter an option.*

Part   Use this mode to sketch, edit, and create features.

Drawing   Use this mode to create and edit drawing views.

Note: The default mode for ADMODE is the mode not currently in use.

ADMOVEDIM

ADMOVEDIM allows you to move the dimensions on the drawing while maintaining their association to the drawing view geometry. You must be in Drawing mode. (See ADMODE on page 303.)

Command: **admovedim**
Reattach/<Select dimension>: *Select a dimension or enter* **r**.
Select view to place dimension: *Select a view.*
Location for dimension: *Select a new location for the dimension.*

Reattach   Connects a dimension extension line to a point on a part after moving it.

                   Select extension line: *Select a dimension extension line.*
                   Select attachment point:
                       Select a point on the part to anchor the dimension.

Commands

AutoCAD Designer places dimensions in the first view that allows a display meeting standard drafting practice. Use ADMOVEDIM to move dimensions to subsequent drawing views where they may better define the part or simply move the dimension within the view.

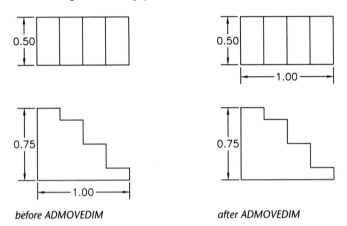

before ADMOVEDIM   after ADMOVEDIM

Figure 5–29. Moving dimensions from the Front View to the Top View

The Reattach option allows you to move dimension extension lines and reattach them to another point on the part. The objective is to eliminate overlaps of dimensions on part edges. For example, the 1.5 dimension extension lines in figure 5–30 overlap the edges of the deep notch in the part.

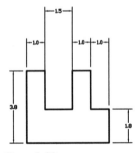

Figure 5–30.

A-32   ADMOVEDIM

You would use the Reattach option to change the extension lines as follows.

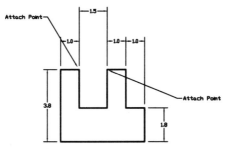

Figure 5–31.

When you reattach dimensions, they must be anchored to a point that results in the same measured distance. The following reattachment is invalid and will be rejected.

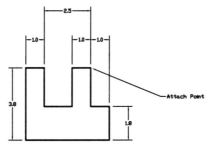

Figure 5–32.

ADMOVELDR

ADMOVELDR moves an annotation leader arrowhead by fixing the start point of the leader line to a new point. You must be in Drawing mode.

Command: **admoveldr**
Select a leader entity: *Select a leader.*
Leader start point: *Pick a new point to which you want the arrowhead to move.*

ADMOVEVIEW

ADMOVEVIEW moves a drawing view, within its restrictions, anywhere on the drawing. You must be in Drawing mode. (See ADMODE on page 303.)

Command: **admoveview**
Select view to move: *Select a view.*
View location: *Pick a new location.*

Orthogonal and auxiliary views have movement restrictions. An orthogonal view must remain aligned to its parent view. An auxiliary view must remain aligned to the edge of the plane selected from the parent view. Moving a parent view also moves all dependent views.

ADNEWPART

ADNEWPART lets you create a new solid part definition while in Part mode.

Command: **adnewpart**

You can't use ADNEWPART to create part geometry. This command initializes a new part and makes it active. The next sketch will build the base feature for the new part.

ADPARAM

ADPARAM lets you create, delete, list, export, and import global parameters.

Command: **adparam**
Create/Delete/List/Import/Export/<eXit>: *Enter an option.*

Global parameters let you define the important, guiding dimensions, factors, and engineering equations that control your design. Use them to set relationships between dimensions on different parts in a single drawing or across a set of AutoCAD drawings.

Chapter 5

Create Lets you define global parameters and assign numeric values or equations to them.

Enter the global parameter name followed by an equal sign (=) and an equation or numeric value.

To set up global parameters for controlling the exterior dimensions of an enclosure, you might create the following global parameters:

Length = 22

Width = sqrt(*length*)

Height = 3*length/*width*

See appendix B, "Mathematical Operators," for a list of the mathematical operators you can use with global parameters. Global parameter equations can include other global parameters, but not dimension parameters.

Delete Deletes the specified global parameters from the current drawing. The Delete option deletes parameters from the current drawing only.

List Lists all global parameters defined in the current AutoCAD drawing.

Import Brings the specified global parameter file into the active AutoCAD drawing.

If you have AutoCAD Designer parts in several AutoCAD *.dwg* files that belong to the same project, you can control the dimensions on these parts with the same global parameters. The Import option lets you read a *.prm* file containing a list of global parameters into an unlimited number of AutoCAD drawings. Create *.prm* files with the Export option of this command.

Export Writes the global parameters defined in the current drawing in a text file with the extension *.prm*. All global parameters defined in the AutoCAD drawing are exported.

Exported parameters can be imported into other drawings with the Import option of this command. If you have several AutoCAD *.dwg* files for a project, you can control the part dimensions in these files with the same global parameters.

ADPARAM

A-35

Commands

Linked Parameter Files

Although you can import multiple *.prm* files into an AutoCAD drawing, only the last one imported becomes the linked parameter file. AutoCAD Designer assigns the name of this file to the AutoCAD Designer system variable ADPARFILE.

Whenever you call an AutoCAD drawing, AutoCAD Designer looks for this linked file and updates the stored global parameters in the drawing to match those in the *.prm* file. This feature lets you control all of the drawings for a project with a single set of global parameters.

You can control part dimensions with global parameters defined with ADPARAM and assign them to dimensions with ADMODDIM or ADEDITFEAT. The next time you update after you change a global parameter value or equation, the affected dimensions update.

Global Parameter Names

Standard alphanumeric characters and the underscore (_) are valid characters in parameter names. AutoCAD Designer does not distinguish between upper- and lower-case letters. In AutoCAD Designer, the global parameters **LENGTH** and **length** are identical. Do not use any mathematical operators or dimension parameters (i.e. d1, d2, and so on) as parameter names.

Linking Global Parameters to Dimensions

To link global parameters to dimensions, select a dimension in the active sketch or drawing with ADMODDIM or on the active part with ADEDITFEAT. Then enter an equal sign (=) followed by a global parameter or an equation containing global parameters.

Editing Global Parameters

If you want to change the current value or equation of an existing global parameter, select ADPARAM and re-enter the global parameter using the Create option.

You can also change global parameters as follows:

1. Export the global parameters with ADPARAM.

2. Edit the operating system text file with a text editor.

3. Import the file back into the AutoCAD drawing with the Import option of ADPARAM.

Chapter 5

The format of the *.prm* file is as follows:

parameter_name1=numeric value or equation
parameter_namen=numeric value or equation

You can add, delete, or change the global parameters when editing this file.

ADPARDIM

ADPARDIM lets you dimension the active sketch interactively, creating AutoCAD dimension entities that drive the feature creation parametrically.

AutoCAD Designer drawings can contain two types of dimensions: parametric or feature dimensions, and reference dimensions.

- Parametric dimensions created with ADPARDIM (in Part mode) become the driving dimensions of the part. The part changes when the dimensions change, and vice versa. AutoCAD Designer automatically places parametric dimensions on drawing views. Additional parametric dimensions are created by the feature commands.

- Reference dimensions are created with ADREFDIM while in Drawing mode. These dimensions define, but don't drive, the model geometry. These dimensions update when the geometry changes.

If you want to change the dimension scheme on a drawing, use the ADREFDIM command.

Command: **adpardim**
Select first item: *Select an entity*
Select second item or place dimension: *Select another entity or locate a point to place the dimension.*

If you select an edge, the following prompt appears:

Undo/Hor/Ver/Align/Par/Dimension value <current>: *Enter an option or the dimension value.*

Undo　　　Performs an AutoCAD undo operation.

Hor　　　Changes the newly created dimension to a horizontal dimension.

Commands

Ver	Changes the newly created dimension to a vertical dimension.
Align	Changes the newly created dimension to an aligned dimension.
Par	Changes the newly created dimension to a parallel dimension. This option is available only if selected parallel lines.
Dimension value	Enter the value of the dimension.

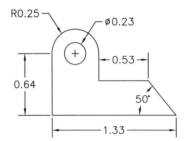

Figure 5–33. Parametric dimensions

If you select an arc or circle, the following prompt appears:

Undo/Dimension value <current>: *Enter an option.*

Adding Dimensions

With a single ADPARDIM command, you can create linear, horizontal, parallel, aligned, vertical, radial, diametral, and angular dimensions. The ADPARDIM command is intuitive, once you understand the guidelines.

Geometry Type and Number of Entities	If you select a line, the dimension measures the distance between the endpoints. If you select an arc, the dimension will be radial.

Chapter 5

If you select a circle, the dimension will be diametral.

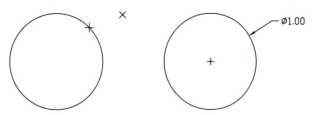

If you select two entities, the cursor location and dimension location determine the type of dimension created.

Cursor Selection

If you select two lines, the dimension created is either the distance or angle between the lines, depending on where you place the cursor when you select the lines.

For linear dimensions, select the lines near the appropriate endpoints.

For angular dimensions, select near the midpoint of the lines.

Dimension Placement

Whether you select a single line or any two entities, the dimension created actually measures between a point on each entity. For all linear dimensions, AutoCAD Designer creates an imaginary box with its opposing corners defined by the two selected points.

Where you place the dimension determines whether you have a linear (aligned), horizontal, or vertical dimension.

Commands

Aligned   Specify anywhere within the imaginary box to create a linear dimension.

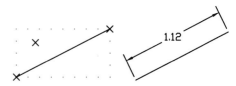

Vertical   Specify outside of the imaginary box to the right or left to create a vertical dimension.

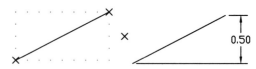

Horizontal   Specify outside of the imaginary box above or below to create a horizontal dimension.

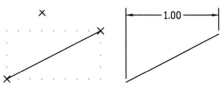

Angular   Specify near the midpoint of two non-parallel lines to create an angular dimension.

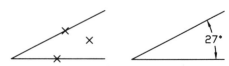

If you select two entities, the imaginary box is created between a point on one of the entities and a point on the other. If an arc or circle is selected, the center point is selected. If a line is selected, the endpoint nearest the selection is selected.

Chapter 5

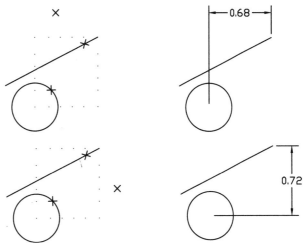

Par Creates a dimension between two parallel lines. This dimension requires two pick points.

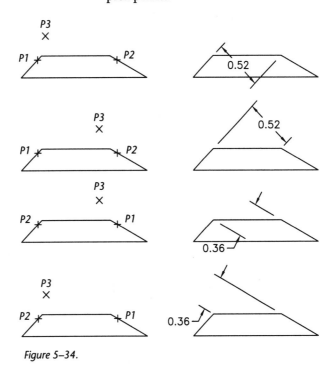

Figure 5-34.

Commands

ADPARTIN

ADPARTIN reads a part or parts from another file into the current file. See chapter 1, "Fundamentals," for more information on importing and exporting files.

Command: **adpartin**
Enter file name: *Enter a file name.*
Select insert point: *Select the location for the imported part or parts.*

ADPARTIN reads in AutoCAD Designer parts only. No drawings are transferred.

ADPARTOUT

ADPARTOUT saves the selected part(s) in a separate file. See chapter 1, "Fundamentals," for more information on importing and exporting files.

Command: **adpartout**
Enter file name: *Enter a file name.*
Select insert point: *Select the insertion point.*
Select parts to write out.
Select objects: *Select part(s).*

ADPARTOUT writes out AutoCAD Designer parts only. No drawings are transferred.

ADPARTVIEW

ADPARTVIEW changes the view orientation in Part mode. See ADMODE on page 303.

Command: **adpartview**
View Option Front/Right/Left/Top/Bottom/Isometric/<Sketch>: *Enter an option.*

The first six view types on the ADPARTVIEW menu are standard plane views—Front, Right, Left, Top, Bottom, and Isometric. All views are aligned to the AutoCAD World Coordinate System (WCS) so that the Front view is parallel to the WCS *XY* plane.

Chapter 5

The Sketch option aligns the view with the active sketch plane, which is equivalent to setting the view to the User Coordinate System (UCS) *XY* plane.

ADPATH

ADPATH creates an active sketch by solving the AutoCAD 2D geometry and dimensions on the active sketch plane. ADPATH is nearly identical to ADPROFILE except that the geometry may be open (see figure 5–36 for an example of an open path). ADPATH is only used to create paths for Sweep features.

Paths are used in Sweep features only to describe the trajectory that the profile sweeps along. To create a sweep using ADPATH, create a path, place a Sweep Profile work plane on a point on the path, and place the sketch plane on this work plane. Then sketch a profile on the sketch plane. The ADSWEEP command asks you to select the path and profile. Then it sweeps that profile along the path.

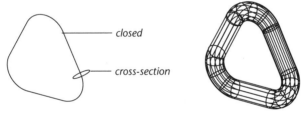

Figure 5–35. Circle swept along closed path

Command: **adpath**
Select objects for sketch: *Select the 2D geometry.*
Specify start point of path: *Select near the end point of an arc or line.*

Figure 5–36. Specifying the start point for a path

The geometry used as the boundaries of the path can be the 2D entities lines, non-spline fit polylines, arcs, and circles.

Commands

Sketch Mode (ADSKMODE)

How AutoCAD Designer treats the selected geometry depends on whether the ADSKMODE variable is 0 or 1. When ADSKMODE is 1, AutoCAD Designer applies constraint rules to your rough sketch. Based on your sketch, the constraint manager tries to apply certain constraints; vertical, horizontal, tangencies, parallelism, and so on. Upon applying these constraints, AutoCAD Designer moves the geometry to reflect the rules the constraint manager just applied. When AutoCAD Designer solves a sketch, it moves the geometry to reflect the constraint rules it applied.

When ADSKMODE is 0, AutoCAD Designer assumes the sketch is precise—that a line drawn at 3.65 degrees is meant to be at 3.65 degrees—and doesn't move geometry.

Note: By default, ADSKMODE is 1.

ADRULEMODE also affects how AutoCAD Designer treats the selected geometry. If ADRULEMODE is off, AutoCAD Designer does not apply constraints other than joining endpoints. By default, ADRULEMODE is on.

Constraining Sketches

ADPATH applies logical geometric constraints to the selected 2D geometric entities. ADPATH does not apply constraints between the sketch geometry and any existing AutoCAD Designer part edges, work plane, or work axes. You must apply these constraints with ADADDCON and add dimensions with ADPARDIM.

As you add constraints and dimensions to the sketch, AutoCAD Designer reports the constraint status. Continue dimensioning and constraining the sketch until it is fully constrained. When a sketch is constrained completely, all subsequent updates react predictably.

See chapter 1, "Fundamentals," for more information on constraints.

AutoCAD Designer Variables

Several AutoCAD Designer variables affect the ADPATH command.

- ADSKMODE controls whether AutoCAD Designer assumes a sketch to be precise or rough.

- ADSKANGTOL controls the angular tolerance within which AutoCAD Designer applies constraint rules.

- ADRULEMODE controls whether AutoCAD Designer automatically applies constraints.

Chapter 5

The AutoCAD pickbox size determines the distance tolerance for applying constraints.

Note: Occasionally geometry creation or trimming creates geometry too small to be visible. If you select this geometry for ADPATH, AutoCAD Designer's solution process may be disrupted. Make sure the number of selected entities listed matches the number of entities you see on screen.

ADPLNDSP

ADPLNDSP is a toggle that displays or hides work planes on the active part.

Command: **adplndsp**
ON/OFf: *Enter an option.*

ON   Displays all work planes in every viewport.

OFf   Prompts to specify the work planes to hide.

Select/<All>: *Enter an option or press* ⏎

All   Hides all work planes.

Select   Prompts to select work planes. Hides selected work planes.

Work planes have many uses in AutoCAD Designer—for example, they are used for locating sketch planes and acting as cutting planes for cross-sectional views. Work planes can clutter up the part display, so you may want to turn off their display when you aren't using them.

ADPROFILE

ADPROFILE creates an active sketch by solving the 2D geometry, model edges, sketch planes, work axes, and dimensions you select. These sketches can be used as cross-sections (or profiles) to create solids from extrusions, revolutions, and sweeps. The sketch for the profile must be closed.

Command: **adprofile**
Select objects for sketch: *Select the 2D geometry.*

The geometry used as the boundaries of the path can be 2D AutoCAD entities, work planes perpendicular to the sketch plane, work axes, or model edges.

Sketch Mode (ADSKMODE)

How AutoCAD Designer treats the selected geometry depends on whether the ADSKMODE variable is 0 or 1. When ADSKMODE is 1, AutoCAD Designer applies constraint rules to your rough sketch. Based on your sketch, the constraint manager tries to apply certain constraints; vertical, horizontal, tangencies, parallelism, and so on. Upon applying these constraints, AutoCAD Designer moves the geometry to reflect the rules the constraint manager just applied. When AutoCAD Designer solves a sketch, it moves the geometry to reflect the constraint rules.

When ADSKMODE is 0, AutoCAD Designer assumes the sketch is precise—that a line drawn at 3.65 degrees is meant to be at 3.65 degrees. It doesn't move geometry.

Note: By default, ADSKMODE is 1.

ADRULEMODE also affects how AutoCAD Designer treats the selected geometry. If ADRULEMODE is off, AutoCAD Designer does not apply constraints other than joining endpoints. By default, ADRULEMODE is on.

Constraining Sketches

ADPROFILE applies logical geometric constraints to the selected 2D entities. ADPROFILE doesn't apply constraints between the sketch geometry and any existing part, edges, work planes, or work axes that aren't part of the sketch. You can apply constraints with ADADDCON and add dimensions with ADPARDIM.

AutoCAD Designer reports the constraint status of a sketch as you add constraints and dimensions. Continue dimensioning and constraining the sketch until it is fully constrained. When a sketch is constrained completely, all subsequent updates react predictably.

See chapter 1, "Fundamentals," for more information on constraints.

AutoCAD Designer Variables

Several AutoCAD Designer variables affect the ADPROFILE command.

- ADSKMODE controls whether AutoCAD Designer assumes a sketch to be precise or rough.

Chapter 5

- ADSKANGTOL controls the angular tolerance within which AutoCAD Designer applies constraint rules.
- ADRULEMODE controls whether AutoCAD Designer automatically applies constraints.

The AutoCAD pickbox size determines the distance tolerance for applying constraints.

Note: Occasionally geometry creation or trimming creates geometry too small to be visible. If you select this geometry for ADPATH, AutoCAD Designer's solution process may be disrupted. Make sure the number of selected entities listed matches the number of entities you see on the screen.

ADSHOWCON identifies zero length lines and reports them when displaying all constraints.

ADPTDSP

ADPTDSP is a toggle that displays the work points on the active part. You must display work points to edit them with ADEDITFEAT or to place holes in them with ADHOLE.

Command: **adptdsp**
OFf/<ON>: *Enter an option.*

The work points display if ADPTDSP is on.

Work points are only useful for placing holes in parts. The ADHOLE command is intended to provide a fast tool for creating the most common placements of holes, such as those created using the From Edges and Concentric options. When the placement of a hole is more unusual, such as at the intersection of two work planes, you can sketch and constrain a work point on which to place the hole.

ADREFDIM

ADREFDIM creates a reference dimension on geometry in a drawing view. Reference dimensions may be used to supplement or replace the dimensioning scheme used to create the part.

AutoCAD Designer drawings can contain two types of dimensions: parametric or feature dimensions, and reference dimensions.

Commands

- Parametric dimensions created with ADPARDIM (in Part mode) become the driving dimensions of the part; the part changes when the dimensions change, and vice versa. Parametric dimensions, such as the depth of an extrusion or the angle of a revolution, are also automatically created by the commands on the Feature submenu. AutoCAD Designer automatically places part dimensions on drawing views. The feature commands create additional parametric dimensions.
- Reference dimensions are created with ADREFDIM while in Drawing mode. These dimensions define, but don't drive, the model geometry. These dimensions update when the geometry changes.

Command: **adrefdim**
Select first item: *Select an item.*
Select second item of place dimension: *Select another item or locate a point to place the dimension.*
Undo/Hor/Ver/Align/Par/Ref/Basic/Placement point: *Enter an option or a new value for the dimension.*

Undo	Performs an AutoCAD undo operation.
Hor	Creates a horizontal dimension.
Ver	Creates a vertical dimension.
Align	Creates an aligned dimension.
Par	Creates a parallel dimension.
Ref	Creates a reference dimension.
Basic	Creates a basic dimension by placing a rectangle around the dimension value.
Placement point	Moves the created dimension to the new location.

Once you have created reference dimensions, use ADDIMATT to change the attributes (see page 285).

Adding Dimensions

With a single ADREFDIM command, you can create linear, horizontal, parallel, aligned, vertical, radial, diametral and angular dimensions as in ADPARDIM. For a description of how to add reference dimensions, see ADPARDIM on page 309. The ADREFDIM command is intuitive, once you understand the guidelines.

Chapter 5

ADREVOLVE

ADREVOLVE creates a revolved solid feature from the active profile.

Figure 5–37. Revolved feature with mesh representation

Command: **adrevolve**
Select axis of revolution: *Select the axis.*

You must specify an axis about which to revolve the profile. Use the following entities for axes:

- A model edge
- A work axis
- A sketched line included in the sketch profile. If the line is not part of the profile boundary, it must be a linetype other than those associated to the ADSKSTYLE system variable.

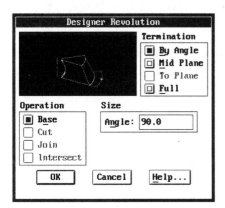

Figure 5–38. Designer Revolution dialogue box

Commands

Termination		Determines how the revolution is ended.
	By angle	Revolves the profile to the specified angle.
	Mid Plane	Revolves the profile equally in both directions, terminating at the specified overall angle.
	To Plane	Defines the specified planar face or work plane to end the revolve operation.
	Full	Revolves the profile 360 degrees.
Operation		Determines the Boolean operation of the revolution.
	Base	Adds material, creating the first feature in a part.
	Cut	Selects the type of cut to remove material from the active part.
	Join	Add material to the active part. Select the type of join.
	Intersect	Creates a new feature from the shared volume of the existing part and the revolved feature.
Size		Enter the value for the angle of revolution.

AutoCAD Designer uses AutoCAD layers to control the display of sketch geometry and dimensions. Whenever a sketch is turned into a feature with ADREVOLVE, ADEXTRUDE, or ADSWEEP, AutoCAD Designer places the solid part and new feature on the current layer. AutoCAD Designer hides the sketch geometry and dimensions for the feature on the AD_FRZ layer so they can be redisplayed by ADEDITFEAT.

Warning: Don't edit the contents of this layer. Doing so can permanently destroy or corrupt the modeling information in your drawing.

ADSATIN

ADSATIN reads a *.sat* format file (ACIS) into AutoCAD Designer.

Command: **adsatin**
Enter .SAT file name (including extension): *Enter the file name.*

Chapter 5

AutoCAD Designer assigns each ACIS body a part ID as it is read in. You can use these bodies as base features. Only ACIS solid bodies are converted. Wire bodies are ignored.

ADSATOUT

ADSATOUT writes an AutoCAD Designer file in standard *.sat* format (ACIS).

Command: **adsatout**

File name: *Enter a name for the file.*

ADSETTINGS

ADSETTINGS lets you set the AutoCAD Designer system variables. For a complete description of these variables, see appendix A, "System Variables."

Command: **adsettings**

You can access the following AutoCAD Designer command or system variables from the ADSETTINGS dialogue box.

Figure 5-39. Designer Settings dialogue box

Commands

Sketch Settings Set the following variable settings:

Rule mode When Rule mode is off, manually apply constraints. ADRULEMODE

Sketch mode When Sketch mode is off, AutoCAD Designer assumes the sketch is precise. ADSKMODE

Angular Tolerance Controls the tolerance angle for constraints. ADSKANGTOL

Pickbox size Sets the size of the pickbox, which affects the tolerances within which constraints are applied. Use the slider to specify the size you want.

Figure 5–40. Pickbox Size dialogue box

Constraint display height Controls the height of displayed constraint symbols on the active sketch. Use the slider to specify the size you want.

Figure 5–41. Constraint Display Size dialogue box

Sketch Linetype Defines the linetype for the path or profile boundary.

Click the Drawing Settings button to set system variables for Drawing mode.

Chapter 5

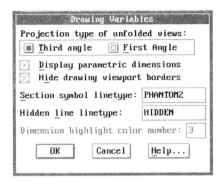

Figure 5–42. Drawing Variables dialogue box

Projection type The ADPROJTYPE variable controls the projection method used to unfold orthographic and auxiliary drawing views. The default setting is the third angle projection. (This method is commonly used in the United States. The first angle projection is used in the United Kingdom.)

Display parametric dimensions The ADREUSEDIM variable sets the automatic display of parametric dimensions. This setting doesn't affect existing views. The default setting is on.

Hide drawing viewport borders The ADBORDER variable sets the display of view borders for existing and new views. The default setting is off.

Section symbol linetype ADSECLTYPE sets the linetype for section lines on the parent view of a cross-section. This setting doesn't affect existing views.

Hidden line linetype ADHIDTYPE sets the linetype for hidden lines in a view. This setting doesn't affect existing views.

ADSHOWACT

ADSHOWACT highlights the active part, sketch, or sketch plane.

Command: **adshowact**
PArt/Sketch plane/<PRofile>: *Enter an option.*

PArt Highlights the active part and reports its part ID.

ADSHOWACT

A-53

Commands

    Sketch Plane   Highlights the active sketch plane, if one exists.

    PRofile   Highlights the active sketch, if one exists.

    Note: By default, most AutoCAD Designer commands act on the active part or sketch.

ADSHOWCON

ADSHOWCON displays the constraint symbols on the active sketch. This display helps you understand the constraint status and assists you in fully constraining the sketch.

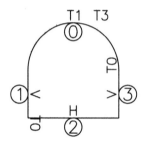

Figure 5–43. Constraints

Command: **adshowcon**
All/Select/Next/<exit>: *Enter an option.*

All	Displays constraints on all entities in the active sketch set.
Select	Displays constraints on entities you select.
Next	Displays constraints on the specified entities one at a time. The following prompt appears:

Select Constraint/exit/<Next>: *Enter an option.*

    Select Constraint   Lets you display constraint partners interactively. If a line is collinear with another line picking the C# symbol highlights the collinear line.

AutoCAD Designer numbers each entity in the sketch and places the constraint symbols for the constraints controlling each line, arc, and

Chapter 5

circle near the center of the entity. Zoom in and out to see the constraints better. The following table lists the constraint symbols:

Symbol	Constraint
H	Horizontal
V	Vertical
L	Perpendicular
P	Parallel
C	Collinear
N	Concentric
J	Projected
R	Same as Radius
T	Tangent
X	Same as *X*
Y	Same as *Y*

You can control the display height of the constraints with the AutoCAD Designer variable ADCONDSPSZ. Use ADSETTINGS to modify this variable.

Note: The join constraint does not display.

ADSKPLN

ADSKPLN sets the sketch plane location and its *XY* axis orientation as you specify. This plane is where you sketch the next feature profile or path on the active part.

Command: **adskpln**

Xy/Yz/Zx/Ucs/<Select work plane or planar face>:
  Enter an option or select the planar face or work plane.

X/Y/Z/<Select work axis or straight edge>:
  Enter an option or select an axis or edge.

Rotate/<Accept>: *Accept the displayed orientation of the UCS or Rotate to see other orientations.*

Commands

The sketch plane is not a displayable entity. The sketch plane is an infinite plane upon which AutoCAD Designer expects the next feature to be sketched. You must create the sketch plane before you create a sketch with ADPROFILE or ADPATH. See "Create a Sketch Plane" in Chapter 1, "Fundamentals," for more information.

Sketches for base feature do not require an active sketch plane. The *X* and *Y* axes orientation of the active sketch plane determines the vertical and horizontal constraint orientation.

Pick Toggling

AutoCAD Designer has picking methods that supplement AutoCAD picking. This is because AutoCAD Designer parts get complicated quickly and picking may be difficult. AutoCAD Designer picking methods are employed when you select features or faces on AutoCAD Designer parts in Part mode. For example, when you use the ADSKPLN command and are prompted to pick a planar face, AutoCAD Designer face picking is employed.

These picking methods use toggling, which means that from a single pick, many possibilities are identified. AutoCAD Designer lets you toggle through all of these possibilities one by one until you get to the entity you want. Every time you pick a face in AutoCAD Designer, the best choice highlights first and AutoCAD Designer prompts: Next/<Accept>. If you enter **n**, AutoCAD Designer highlights the next choice. However, the goal of AutoCAD Designer picking is to get the right choice on the very first pick.

Hints for Successful Feature Selection:

1. If the face is on the front of the part, pick right on the face, keeping the pickbox away from any edges.

2. If the face is near the back of the part, pick on an edge. Only two faces can ever share an edge so you have a 50% chance of getting the correct face first. AutoCAD Designer will pick the most recently created face first.

ADSWEEP

ADSWEEP creates a solid feature defined by a planar cross-section (profile) swept along a planar trajectory (path). You must create two sketches for a solid Sweep feature.

Chapter 5

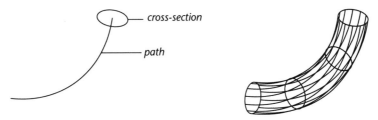

Figure 5–44. Circular cross-section swept along path

Command: **adsweep**
Select sweep path: *Select an entity in the path sketch.*
Select sweep cross section profile: *Select an entity in the profile sketch.*
Parallel/<Normal>: *Enter an option.*

Parallel	Creates a solid Sweep maintaining the profile parallel to the profile sketch plane.
<Normal>	Creates a solid Sweep with a profile normal to the sweep path. This option lets you specify a draft angle if both the path and the profile contain lines and polylines only (no arcs or circles), and the path is perpendicular to the profile.

Draft angle (positive tapers out) <0>: *Enter a positive or negative number.*

A negative values creates a negative draft. The default value of 0 creates no taper. After you choose **Parallel** or **Normal**, if the Sweep feature you are creating is for a new feature of the existing part, AutoCAD Designer prompts you with the following:

Cut/Join/<Intersect>: *Enter an option.*

Cut	Removes material from the active part.
Join	Adds material to the active part.
Intersect	Creates a new feature from the shared volume of the existing part and the Sweep feature.

Commands

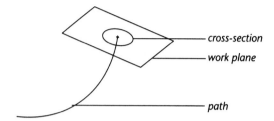

Figure 5–45. Profile sweep

The profile's sketch plane depends on the path's sketch plane. If the path changes, causing the endpoint on which the profile was sketched to move, the profile moves also.

AutoCAD Designer uses AutoCAD layers to control the display of sketch geometry and dimensions. Whenever a sketch is turned into a feature with ADREVOLVE, ADEXTRUDE, or ADSWEEP, AutoCAD Designer places the solid part and new feature on the current layer. AutoCAD Designer hides the sketch geometry and dimensions for the feature on the ADP_FRZ layer so they can be redisplayed by ADEDITFEAT.

Warning: Don't edit the contents of this layer. Doing so can permanently destroy or corrupt the modeling information in your drawing.

Before you use ADSWEEP, you need a path and profile from which to create the swept feature. Use the following steps to create a valid combination of path and profile:

Chapter 5

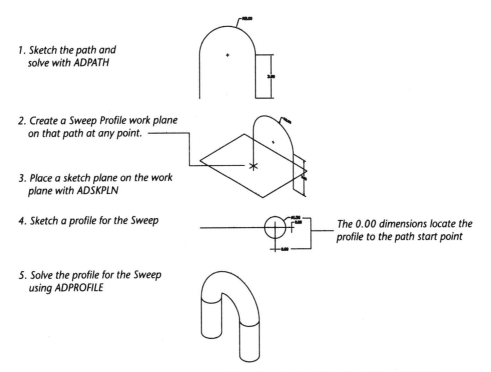

Figure 5–46. Steps to create a valid combination of path and profile for ADSWEEP

ADTHAWDIM

ADTHAWDIM displays drawing dimensions frozen with ADFRZDIM.

Command: **adthawdim**
Thaw dimensions View/<All>: *Enter an option.*

View Thaws frozen dimensions by view.

All Thaws all frozen dimensions.

Commands

ADUPDATE

ADUPDATE regenerates the active part or drawing using any new dimension values or changed sketches.

Command: **adupdate**

If Drawing mode is on, AutoCAD Designer processes any changes to dimension values on the active part by updating all drawing views and the active part.

If Part mode is on, AutoCAD Designer processes any changes to dimension values on the active part by updating the part geometry.

If the part is currently in rollback state, (that is, if you have just edited a feature sketch using the Sketch option of ADEDITFEAT) ADUPDATE updates the part and rolls it back to its completed state.

ADVER

ADVER displays the release number of the AutoCAD Designer software.

Command: **adver**
ADVER = "R1.1" (read only)

ADVIEW

ADVIEW creates any of the following drawing view types from an AutoCAD Designer solid model: base view, auxiliary view, orthogonal view, isometric view, or detail view. Each view is numbered consecutively as you create it.

AutoCAD Designer creates the following two layers for a view:

- ADV_#_HID for hidden geometry
- ADV_#_VIS for visible geometry

Warning: Don't edit the contents of these layers. Doing so can permanently destroy or corrupt the modeling information in your drawing.

Command: **adview**

Chapter 5

AutoCAD Designer creates parts in AutoCAD model space (TILEMODE is on). Drawing views, parametric dimensions, and reference dimensions are in paper space.

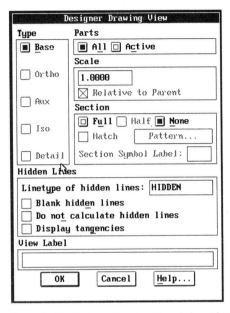

Figure 5–47. Designer Drawing View dialogue box

Type	Creates the type of view you specify. For more complete descriptions of these view types, see "View Types" on page 335.

	Base	Creates a general view of a drawing without a predefined orientation.
	Ortho	Creates an orthogonal mechanical plan view.
	Aux	Creates a view of the specified face of the part.
	Iso	Creates an isometric view.
	Detail	Creates an enlarged view to show small details.

Parts	Determines whether all parts or only the active part appears in the drawing view.
Scale	Sets the scale for the drawing view.

ADVIEW A-61

Commands

Section	\multicolumn{2}{l}{Select the cross-section type you want for the view. Cross-sections are available for base, orthographic, and auxiliary views only. For more information on cross-sections, see "Cross-sectional Views" on page 337.}

      Full   Displays a full section.

      Half   Displays a half section.

      None   Doesn't display any sections.

      Hatch   Automatically cross-hatches the section view.

      Pattern   Displays the Hatch Option dialogue box. This is identical to the Hatch Option dialogue box for AutoCAD BHATCH.

      Section Symbol Label   Enter the symbol you want to use for the section.

Hidden Line   Removes hidden lines from the view.

      Linetype of hidden lines   Sets the linetype for the hidden lines.

      Blank hidden lines   Represses hidden line display.

      Display tangencies   Lets you change the display of tangent edges in the view.

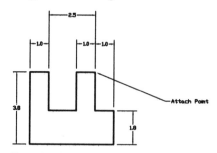

Figure 5–48.

      Do not calculate hidden lines   Represses hidden line processing.

View Label   Enter text for the view label.

ADVIEW

Chapter 5

View Types

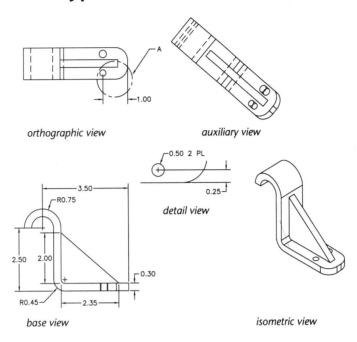

Figure 5-49. Different view types

Base

Base views are general views of a drawing with no predefined orientation. The base view is parallel to the planar face or work plane chosen during view creation. You can align the *XY* axes for the view during view creation as well. Base views do not depend on other views for any of their attributes. You can control the following attributes for base views: scale, orientation, cross-section type, view label, and hidden line display. When you use the **Base** option, AutoCAD Designer displays the following prompts:

Xy/Yz/Zx/Ucs/<Select work plane or planar face>:

X/Y/Z/<Select work axis or straight edge>:

Rotate/<Accept>:

AutoCAD Designer switches to paper space and displays the following prompt:

View center:

AutoCAD Designer removes hidden lines from the view and displays the view with dimensions and labels.

Commands

Aux

Auxiliary views are true size views of any face on the part. Typically, true size views of these faces cannot be created with an orthographic view.

Select the true size face by picking an edge bounding that face in the parent view. The parent view is typically perpendicular to the face. The parent view can be any view type that was on the drawing prior to the auxiliary view's creation.

You can place the view to one or the other side of the selected edge. AutoCAD Designer creates a view perpendicular to that edge.

Auxiliary view attributes are determined from the parent view. The scale is the same as in the parent view and the orientation is derived from the edge you select from the parent view. When you use the Aux option, AutoCAD Designer displays the following prompt:

Select a straight edge in the parent view:
Select second point or <RETURN> to use the selected edge:

This edge selection determines the auxiliary plane from which the auxiliary view is derived.

Location for auxiliary view:

The cursor restricts this placement to the two possible projections.

Once the view location is final, AutoCAD Designer removes hidden lines from the view and displays the view with dimensions and labels.

Ortho

Ortho views are standard orthogonal mechanical plan views derived from a parent view. Ortho view attributes are determined from the parent view. The scale is the same as in the parent view and the orientation must be a valid orthographic projection from the parent view. The projection follows the third or first hand rule as defined by the ADPROJTYPE system variable, as described in appendix A, "System Variables." When you use the Ortho option, AutoCAD Designer displays the following prompts:

Select parent view:
Location for orthographic view:

Chapter 5

The cursor restricts this placement to the four possible projections. Once the view location is finalized, AutoCAD Designer performs a hidden line removal operation on the view and displays the view with dimensions and labels.

Iso

Isometric views are views in which the principal axes of the parent view are equally foreshortened. In isometric view, the X, Y, and Z axes of the parent view appear to be separated by 120 degrees, as if you were viewing a cube along a diagonal. You can derive four different isometric views from an existing view, corresponding to the four diagonals of a cube. By picking the location of the isometric view relative to the parent view, you establish which of these four types of isometric view is generated. You can move and scale an isometric view independently.

Although you can not generate a cross-section during isometric view creation, you can create an isometric view of a sectioned parent view. The sectioned part appears in the isometric view.

Detail

Detail views are enlarged views of the part. These views show small details and dimensions. Detail views can be scaled differently from the parent view. Their scale can be absolute or it can be a multiple of the parent view's scale. The detail view maintains the same orientation as the parent view. You can't cut a cross-section while creating a detail view.

Cross-sectional Views

The cutting plane for cross-sections is determined by work planes, or a point on the parent view. The projection type (controlled by the ADPROJTYPE system variable) determines which portion of the object is kept. For either projection type, the cutting arrows on the parent view point away from the discarded material.

Commands

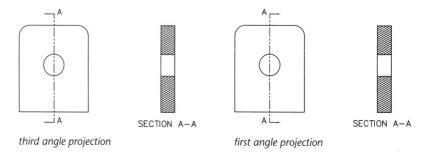

third angle projection   *first angle projection*

Figure 5–50. Arrow display for cross-sectional views

When the section type is Full, AutoCAD Designer discards one half of the part. For Half sections, only one quadrant of the part is discarded. A second cutting plane is required to determine the four quadrants of the part.

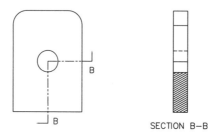

Figure 5–51. Half Section

Work Planes as Cutting Planes

If you create a cross-section in a Base view, you must select a work plane to orient the view. This work plane acts as the cutting plane. You cannot create Half sections or use the point cutting plane option when you create Base views.

When you create cross-sections in Ortho and Aux views using the work plane option, you select the work planes from the parent view. A single work plane, parallel to the new view, is required for a Full section. For Half sections, you select two mutually perpendicular work planes to determine the quadrant to remove.

Points as Cutting Planes

If the Point option is chosen for cross-sections in Ortho and Aux views, you pick a point in the parent view. For Full sections, AutoCAD Designer creates a virtual cutting plane through this point, parallel to the new view. For Half sections, AutoCAD Designer creates two virtual

Chapter 5

cutting planes, one parallel to the new view and one normal to it. Both intersect at the selected point.

ADWORKAXIS

ADWORKAXIS creates a work axis at the centerline of the selected cylindrical, conical, or toroidal surface. AutoCAD Designer places work axes, work planes, and work points on the ADP_WORK layer.

Warning: Don't edit the contents of these layers. Doing so can permanently destroy or corrupt the modeling information in your drawing.

Command: **adworkaxis**
Select cylindrical face: *Select the curved surface(s).*

Cylindrical, conical, and toroidal surfaces result from the following operations:

- Revolved arcs and lines
- Extruded circles and arcs with and without draft
- Holes
- Fillets on straight line edges

You can dimension or constrain new sketches to the work axes and create work planes through the work axis.

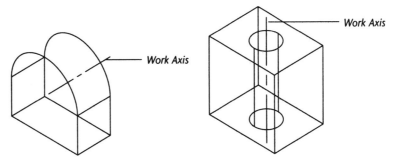

Figure 5–52. Work axis display

ADAXISDSP controls axis display, specify on to display all axes.

ADWORKAXIS A-67

Commands

ADWORKPLN

ADWORKPLN creates a construction plane on the active part. AutoCAD Designer places work axes, work planes, and work points on the ADP_WORK layer.

Warning: Don't edit the contents of these layers. Doing so can permanently destroy or corrupt the modeling information in your drawing.

Command: **adworkpln**

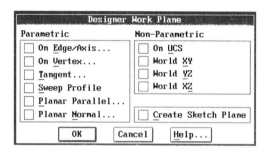

Figure 5–53. Designer Work Plane dialogue box

Parametric Determines the constraints for a parametric work plane.

        On Edge/Axis Constrains the work plane to the specified linear model edge or work axis.

        On Vertex Constrains the work plane to lie on the specified vertex of the part.

        Tangent Constrains the work plane so it is tangent to a curved surface. There are two solutions for tangent placements, even if one of the surface options falls on a trimmed surface. The default tangency is the one closest to the pick point.

        Sweep Profile Constrains the work plane so it is normal to the specified path at the selected endpoint.

	Planar Parallel	Constrains the work plane so it is parallel to the selected plane.
	Planar Normal	Constrains the work plane so it is normal to the selected plane.
Non-Parametric		Determines the constraints for non-parametric work planes.
	On UCS	Constrains the work plane to the UCS (User Coordinate System).
	World XY	Constrains the work plane to the *XY* plane of the WCS.
	World YZ	Constrains the work plane to the *YZ* plane of the WCS.
	World XZ	Constrains the work plane to the XZ plane of the WCS.

Parametric Work Planes

Parametric work planes are parametrically attached to the edges, axes, vertices, and surfaces of a part. When you change the part geometry, the location of the work plane changes

When you construct a parametric work plane, you must fully constrain its relationship to the active part. You may combine the following parametric work plane options to define a work plane:

- On Edge/Axis
- On Vertex
- Tangent
- Planar Parallel
- Planar Normal
- Planar Angle

When you select any of these options, a second dialogue box appears. Now you can choose subsequent options. For example, you can specify On Edge/Axis and On Vertex to define a work plane.

ADWORKPLN

Commands

Your selection of edges, axes, vertices, and planes must identify a unique, complete, valid set of constraints for any parametric work plane. An example of an invalid work plane definition is to specify On Edge/Axis and On Edge/Axis and then select two skewed lines. AutoCAD Designer could not create a work plane from these specifications. See figure 5–54.

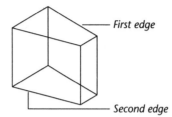

Figure 5–54. Invalid work planes. The edges are skewed

A non-unique work plane definition would be to specify **On Edge/Axis** and **Planar Normal** constraints and select the axis of a cylinder and the end cap of the cylinder as shown in figure 5–55.

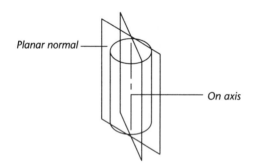

Figure 5–55. Non-unique solution

Since there are an infinite number of work planes that satisfy these constraints, AutoCAD Designer could not create a work plane.

Two additional parametric work plane options are available:

Offset The planar work plane is offset the distance you specify.

On 3 Vertices The work plane on the three specified vertices of the part.

The swept profile completely defines a work plane and is not used in combination with the constraints.

Nonparametric Work Planes

Nonparametric work planes have fixed locations relative to part geometry. Because they have no links to geometry, the work planes do not change orientation when the part changes shape or size. There are two types of nonparametric work planes: UCS work planes and WCS work planes.

UCS Work Planes

The On UCS work plane is a fixed plane placed on the *XY* plane of the current UCS. This work plane is not parametrically associated with part geometry. If the geometry changes during updating, the work plane does not change. During AutoCAD transforms, the On UCS plane transforms along with the part geometry.

WCS Work Planes

World XY, World YZ, and World XZ are static work planes placed on the WCS *XY* (z=0), *YZ* (x=0), and *XZ* (y=0). These planes are fixed with respect to part geometry. During AutoCAD transform operations, the Part_ planes transform along with the part geometry.

Pick Toggling

AutoCAD Designer has picking methods that supplement AutoCAD picking. This is because AutoCAD Designer parts get complicated quickly and picking may be difficult. AutoCAD Designer picking methods are employed when you select features or faces on AutoCAD Designer parts in Part mode. For example, when you use ADWRKPLN and are prompted to pick a planar face, AutoCAD Designer face picking is employed.

These picking methods use toggling, which means that from a single pick, many possibilities are identified. AutoCAD Designer lets you toggle through all of these possibilities one by one until you get to the entity you want. Every time you pick a face in AutoCAD Designer, the best choice highlights first and AutoCAD Designer prompts: Next/<Accept>. If you enter **n**, AutoCAD Designer highlights the next choice. However, the goal of AutoCAD Designer picking is to get the right choice on the very first pick.

Commands

Hints for Successful Feature Selection:

1. If the face is on the front of the part, pick the face, keeping the pickbox away from any edges.

2. If the face is near the back of the part, pick on an edge. Only two faces can ever share an edge so you have a 50% chance of getting the correct face first. AutoCAD Designer will pick the most recently created face first.

ADWORKPT

ADWORKPT creates work points used for locating holes. AutoCAD Designer places work axes, work planes, and work points on the ADP_WORK layer.

Warning: Don't edit the contents of this layer. Doing so can permanently destroy or corrupt the modeling information in your drawing.

Command: **adworkpt**

Location on sketch plane: *Specify a location.*

Work points are only useful for placing holes in parts. The ADHOLE command is intended to provide a fast tool for the most common placements of holes, such as those created using the From Edges and Concentric options. When the placement of a hole is more unusual, such as at the intersection of two work planes, you can sketch and constrain a work point on which to place the hole.

There are three steps in the process of creating work points:

1. Create a sketch plane
2. Place the work point
3. Dimension and constrain the work point

Chapter 5

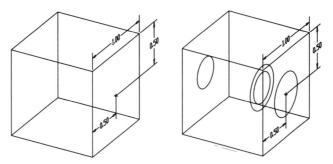

Figure 5–56. Work points

The dimensions on the point remain visible until you use ADPROFILE, ADPATH, or ADWORKPT or place a hole on the work point. Before using the point to place a hole, you can modify work points with ADMODDIM by changing any dimension values used in their placement. Once the point is used to position the hole, use ADEDITFEAT to change the work point's hole location.

Use work points in placing Hole features by using the On Point option in the ADHOLE dialogue box.

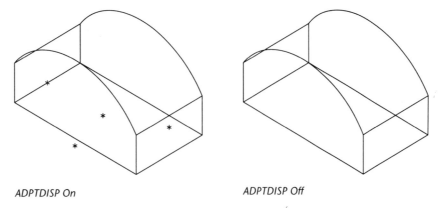

ADPTDISP On   ADPTDISP Off

Figure 5–57. AutoCAD Designer feature with and without work points displayed

Note: Points appear as three perpendicular lines originating from the point center.

The global display variable ADPTDSP turns the display of all work points on and off for the active part.

ADWORKPT

Index

Absolute dimensions, 26
acad.dwg file, 74
adaddcon command, 41, 42, 50, 93
adbonus2.lsp file, 6-7, 125
adchamfer command, 62
Add Dimension option, 10, 26, 28, 45-46, 93, 110, 122, 136, 144
addelcon command, 43
addelview command, 79, 83, 85
addimdsp command, 121
Adding
    annotations to a hole, 82-83
    auxiliary views, 85-86
    a chamfer to an edge, 62-64
    constraints, 41-43
    cross-sections, 83-85
    detail views, 86
    a fillet to an edge, 62, 145-146
    a hole, 12-13, 60-61, 96-99, 142-143
    parametric dimensions to a profile, 9-10, 25-27, 28-30
    reference dimensions to a drawing, 80
    views, 14-15, 72-78
    a work axis, 134
    work points, 143-145
adeditfeat command, 64, 81
adeditview command, 79
adesign.dwg file, 74
adesign.mnx file, 6-7
adextrude command, 59, 95
adfillet command, 62, 145
adhole command, 60, 96, 142, 147
adholenote command, 82
admoddin command, 44, 80
admode command, 72, 80
admovedim command, 82
adparam command, 118, 126, 128, 146
adpardim command, 9-10, 25, 28, 44, 49, 50, 94, 109, 118, 126, 128, 144, 147
adpartview command. 95, 124, 127, 135
adpath command, 120
adprofile command, 8-9, 20, 38, 48, 92, 120, 125
adrefdim command, 80
adrevolve command, 110
adshowcon command, 21, 24, 39, 40, 42, 49, 93

adskpln command, 95
adsweep command, 128
adupdate command, 65, 80, 81, 128
adview command, 72, 75, 83, 85, 86
adworkaxis command, 134
adworkpln command, 134
Algebraic numeric constraint, 4
Aligned linear dimension, 26
Angular dimensions, 27
Annotating a hole, 82-83
Applications option, 56
arcrad global parameter, 118, 119, 122, 128, 139, 141
arc command, 19, 135
Architecture of AutoCAD, 6
Attributes option, 79
AutoCAD
    automatically loading Designer when starting, 6
    basic drawing commands in, 18-19
    changing linetypes in, 47-48
    creating a sketch with, 4
    editing commands in, 78, 82
    erasing in, 41-42
    loading **AutoLisp** routines into, 56
    open architecture of, 6
    opening files in, 40
    plotting a drawing in, 65
    polylines in, 8, 18
    saving drawing files in, 30-31
    viewports in, 56
    zoom command for, 125
AutoLisp routines, 95
    description of, 56
    loading, 56
Auxiliary views, 85-86
    creating, 85-86
    description of, 85

Base operation, 56-57
Base view
    creating, 72-74
    description of, 72
Bi-directional associativity, 13, 71, 80
Blind termination, 57, 59, 98

C (collinear constraint) symbol, 4, 19, 25
CAD (computer-aided design)
    parametric features of, 2-4
    traditional systems for, 1
Chamfer
    adding to a model, 62-64
Chamfer option, 62
Change Dimension option, 44, 80
Changing
    attributes of a view, 79
    constraints, 39-41
    dimensions, 44, 80-81
chprop command, 48
circle command, 19, 125
Collinear (C) constraint, 4, 19, 25
Commands. *See specific commands*
Concentric (N) constraint, 4, 19, 25
Constraints. *See also* Geometric constraints; Parametric dimensions (numeric constraints)
    definition of, 3
Construction geometry
    definition of, 46
    using, to define a profile, 47-51
Continuous linetypes, 47
copy command, 78
Correcting mistakes, using the **Undo** command, 78, 94
Create option (for parameters), 118, 128
Create Sketch Plane option, 124, 143
Create View option, 13, 72, 75, 83, 85
Cross-sectioning
    description of, 83
    procedure for creating, 83-85
    work planes for, 100
Cut operation, 57

Defining global parameters, 118-119, 126
Delete option, 43, 64, 79, 83
Deleting
    constraints, 39-41
    features in a model, 64
    views, 79
Designer. *See also* AutoCAD Designer
    AutoLisp routines, 56
    bi-directional associativity in, 13, 71, 80
    creating a model with, 1-2
    creating a sketch with, 4
    cross-sectioning features of, 83-85
    design process using, 4-6
    drafting features of, 1
    as a feature based CAD system, 2-4, 60
    fundamentals of, 1-15
    global parameters in, 117-118
    loading, 6-7
    model creation features of, 1
    parametric features of, 2-4
    sweep features of, 117
    traditional CAD systems compared with, 1-2
    work features of, 99-105
Designer menu, 6-7
Design process
    overview of, 4-5
    steps in, 5-6
    terminology used with, 3-4
Detail views
    creating, 86
    description of, 86
Dim Display option, 121, 136
Dimensions. *See* Parametric dimensions (numeric constraints); Reference dimensions
Displaying parametric dimensions, 121-122
Drawing commands, in AutoCAD, 18-19
Drawing files
    loading, 74
    opening, 40
    saving, 30-31
Drawing mode, 71-72
Drawings
    adding reference dimensions to, 80
    auxiliary view on, 85-86
    base view on, 72-74
    changing parametric dimensions of, 80-81
    creating views on, 72-78, 85-86
    creating, from a model, 13-15, 71-87
    cross-sections on, 83-85
    detail view on, 86
    editing views on, 78-79
    hole notes on, 82-83
    isometric view on, 77-78
    moving parametric dimensions of, 82
    plotting, 65-66
    prototype files for, 74
    right side view on, 75-76
    top view on, 76-77
.dwg file extension, 30

Edit Feature option, 64, 81
Editing
    features in a model, 64-65
    global parameters, 128-129
    views, 78-79
Engineering design process, 4-6
Equations option, 121
erase command, 41-42, 78, 79

Errors, correcting, using the **Undo** command, 78, 94
Extrude option, 11, 59, 95, 141
Extruding a profile, 11, 56-60, 95, 141-42
    options in, 56-58
    procedure for, 59-60

Files
    for drawing prototypes, 74
    for loading **AutoLisp** routines, 56
    for Loading Designer, 6-7
    opening, 40
    saving, 30-31
Fillet
    adding to a model, 62, 145-146
Fillet option, 62, 145
Fixed point, 9
Fully constrained profile, 9, 30, 38

Geometric constraints
    adding, 41-43
    adding to a sweep path, 121
    applying, on a sketch, 23-25
    changing, 39-41
    construction geometry and, 46-51
    creating a sketch and, 4
    defining a profile using combinations of dimensions and, 45-51
    definition of, 3
    deleting, 39-41, 43-44
    in an overconstrained sketch, 39
    relationships between dimensions and, 38-44
    showing, on a sketch, 21-23
    symbols for, 3-4, 25
    in an underconstrained sketch, 38, 139, 140
    using, 17, 18
    viewing, 39-41
Global parameters
    defining, 118-119, 126, 146-148
    description of, 117-118
    editing, 128-129

H (horizontal constraint) symbol, 4, 18, 25, 41, 49
Hidden linetypes, 47-48
Hole
    adding, 60-61, 96-99, 142-143
    annotating, 82-83
    blind termination option for, 98
    simple exercise for creating, 12-13
Hole Note option, 82
Hole option, 12, 60, 96, 98, 142, 147

Horizontal (H) constraint, 4, 18, 25, 41, 49
Horizontal linear dimension, 26

Intersect operation, 57
Isometric view, 11, 77-78, 127
Iso option, 11, 77, 95, 141

Join operation, 57

L (perpendicular constraint) symbol, 4, 18, 25, 41
Linear dimensions
    adding to a profile, 26
    types of, 26-27
line command, 18-19, 135
Linetypes, 47-48
List option, **adpardim** command, 126
Loading Designer
    automatically, when starting AutoCAD, 6
    steps for, 6-7
Loading files
    for **AutoLisp** routines, 56
    for drawing prototypes, 74

Menu option, 6
Mid Plane termination, 57, 141
Mistakes, correcting, using the **Undo** command, 78, 94
Model. *See* Three-dimensional (3-D) model
Mode option, 72
Modes, switching, 72
Modifying a sketch (model)
    in the design process, 5-6
    simple exercise for, 11-13
move command, 78, 82
Move View option, 79
Moving
    dimensions, 82
    views, 79

N (concentric constraint) symbol, 4, 19, 25
Nonparametric work planes, 100
Numeric constraints. *See also* Parametric dimensions (numeric constraints)
    definition of, 3
    refining a model with, 5
Numeric option, 121

Opening files, 40
Ortho view, 14-15

P (parallel constraint) symbol, 4, 18, 25
Parallel linear dimension, 27

Parameter
    definition of, 3, 55
    global. *See* Global parameters
Parameters option, 121
Parametric dimensions (numeric constraints)
    absolute, 26
    adding to a profile, 9-10, 25-27
    adding to a sketch, 28-30, 126-127
    adding to a sweep path, 121, 122-123
    angular, 27
    changing, 44, 80-81
    defining a profile using combinations of constraints and, 45-51
    definition of, 3, 55-56
    displaying, 121-122
    linear, 26-27
    moving, 82
    relationships between constraints and, 38-44
    relative, 26
    using, 17-18
Parametric feature based CAD systems
    description of, 2-4, 60
Parametric work planes, 100
Part mode, 71
Path, creating, 120
Path option, 120
Perpendicular (L) constraint, 4, 18, 25, 41
Plot command, 65
Plotting a drawing, 65-66
polyline (**pline**) command, 8, 18, 92, 120, 135
Problem definition, and design, 5
Profile. *See also* Two-dimensional (2-D) profile
    adding parametric dimensions to, 9-10, 25-27
    creating, for a sweep, 119, 124-127
    creating, from a sketch, 8-9, 20-27, 92-94, 135-141
    creating a 3-D solid model from, 55-66
    defining, using combinations of constraints and dimensions, 45-51
    definition of, 3
    extruding, to create a model, 11, 56-60, 141-42
    simple exercise for creating, 8-15
    solved (fully constrained), 9, 30, 38
Profile option, 8, 20, 92, 109, 136
Prototypes, drawing files for, 74

R (same radius values constraint) symbol, 4, 19, 25
Ref Dim option, 80

Reference dimensions
    adding to a drawing, 80
    definition of, 80
Refining a sketch, 5
Relative dimensions, 26
Removing constraints, 43-44
Revolved cut, 106
Revolve operation, 110
rotate command, 78

Saving drawing files, 30-31
Scaled to Fit option, 65
Segments option, 108
Show option, 21, 40, 93
Sketch
    adding dimensions to, 28-30, 126-127
    applying constraints to, 23-25
    creating, 5, 18-20, 92, 134-135
    creating a profile from, 8-9, 20-27, 92-94
    definition of, 4
    fixed point on, 9
    modifying, 5-6
    overconstrained, 39
    refining, 5
    showing constraints on, 21-23
    simple exercise for creating, 7-15
    underconstrained, 38, 139, 140
Sketch option, 96, 108, 124, 135, 143
Sketch plane
    creating, 95-96, 124
    creating, on a work plan, 107-108
    creating a semicircular profile on, 108-110
    description of, 95
Sketch Plane option, 95, 107, 124
Sweep
    adding constraints to, 121
    adding parametric dimensions to, 122-123
    building, 119-128
    constraints for, 121
    creating, 119, 128
    creating a work plane for, 123-124
    description of, 117
    profile for, 124-127
Sweep option, 128
Symbols for constraints
    description of use of, 3-4, 18-19
    table listing of, 4, 25

T (tangent constraint) symbol, 4, 18, 25, 41, 49
Termination methods, 57
Terminology, 3-4

Three-dimensional (3-D) model, 1. *See also* Creating a model
    advanced example for, 91-112
    creating 2-D views from, 71-87
Through termination, 57
To plane termination, 57
Top view, 76-77
Two-dimensional (2-D) profile, 1
    creating, from a 3-D model, 71-87
    creating a sketch for, 4, 18-20
    creating a 3-D solid model from, 55-66

Undo command, 78, 94

V (vertical constraint) symbol, 4, 18, 25, 41
Vertical linear dimension, 26
Viewing constraints, 39-41
Viewports, 56, 95
View
    auxiliary, 85-86
    base, 72-74
    changing attributes of, 79
    creating, from a model, 14-15, 72-78
    cross-sectioning, 83-85
    deleting, 79
    detail, 86
    editing, 78-79
    isometric, 11, 77-78
    moving, 79
    right side, 75-76
    top, 76-77

vports command, 95

Work axis
    adding, 134
    creating, 106
    definition of, 99-100
Work Axis option, 106
Work features of Designer, 99-105
Work plane
    constraint options for, 100-1-5
    creating, 106-107
    creating, for a sweep, 119, 123-124
    creating a sketch plane on, 107-108
    definition of, 100
    types of, 100
    uses of, 100
Work Plane option, 106, 123, 134
Work Point option, 144
Work points
    adding, 143-145
    definition of, 99

X (same X coordinates constraint) symbol, 4, 19, 25

Y (same Y coordinates constraint) symbol, 4, 19, 25

zoom command, 125, 135, 144, 145